P9-DID-336

Robert Gilmour LeTourneau.
Photo by Harris & Ewing, Washington

MOVING
HEAVEN AND EARTH

Moving
Heaven and Earth

R. G. Le TOURNEAU

Inventor, Designer, Manufacturer, Preacher

by

DONALD F. ACKLAND

THE IVERSEN-FORD ASSOCIATES

NEW YORK

THE IVERSEN-FORD ASSOCIATES
175 FIFTH AVENUE
NEW YORK 10, N. Y.

First Edition 1949

MADE AND PRINTED IN UNITED STATES BY THE BIGGER PRESS, INC.
NEW YORK

FOREWORD

THIS BOOK is the outcome of a visit to the United States in the summer of 1947, as the guest of Mr. R. G. LeTourneau. In his company I travelled 16,000 miles by air, visiting each of his factories many times, accompanying him to widely-separated towns and cities where he was scheduled to speak, and having unique facilities for observing the work of the LeTourneau Foundation in its varied aspects.

In presenting my story to the American public it may be necessary to state that I have written as an Englishman endeavoring to interpret to English-speaking readers everywhere an outstanding American personality against the contemporary American background. Such an explanation may relieve me of the charge of pedantry, and obviate the necessity for revising in this edition certain distinctively English phrases and idioms.

My thanks are due to many people for the hospitality and courtesy shown to me, and for the ready way in which they co-operated to furnish me with all the information I required. In particular, I acknowledge a debt of gratitude to Mr. LeTourneau himself and to Mrs. LeTourneau, who did so much to make my stay among them happy and memorable. To their family, too, I express my sincere thanks for every kindness shown to me.

The concern for my welfare constantly demonstrated by Dr. Harold Strathearn and Mrs. Strathearn is something I shall ever remember and now appreciatively record. The help received from Mr. Donald M. Taylor, of Peoria, and our fellowship together are matters for happy recollection. To these all I declare my indebtedness—and add to their names a host of kindly men and women who, in innumerable ways, made my American visit an experience of unalloyed pleasure, and contributed toward the success of my task. That I have now made my home among them is perhaps the highest compliment I can pay.

D. F. ACKLAND.

CONTENTS

LIST OF ILLUSTRATIONS

PROLOGUE

La Guardia Field, New York's famous junction of the air, is facing the end of its supremacy. On Long Island, but a few miles away, a competitor is rising, boasting its ultimate superiority even in its incompleteness—ambitiously looking forward to the day when mighty ships of the air will sweep down to its smooth runways, disembarking thousands of travellers from all parts of the world, who will declare as their crowning experience: "I landed at Idlewild."

It was in April, 1942, that this great project of engineering skill was commenced, by which nearly 5,000 acres of marshland are to be transformed into the largest and busiest airport of the Americas, eight times larger than La Guardia. For the conquest of the marshes, millions of cubic yards of sand have been transferred by hydraulic suction from Jamaica Bay and spread ten-feet deep over the site. Then, to bind the sand, special grasses have been planted . . . all to provide the foundation upon which Idlewild will rise.

Soon, many thousands of people will find employment at Idlewild, enabling 30,000 passengers to pass through the airport daily. The twelve—or more—runways which will eventually be laid will be able to receive the biggest planes that take the air. One will extend for 11,200 feet, and two others will measure 10,000 feet.

And for the convenience of passengers a new high-

way will be constructed giving access to the heart of New York City in less than half-an-hour.

But there are no ships of the air at Idlewild as I write. They are of the future, and the present belongs to strange, slow-moving mammoths whose element is not the sky but the earth. Men perched mahout-like on these monsters' backs are forcing them to their will. With a roar they thrust their snouts high into the air, lurch forward, shaking and tearing the ground in their fury, scooping it into their cavernous mouths. Ton after ton they consume in the insatiability of their appetites; and when they have all they can hold, see them triumphantly lift their laden bodies from the earth, lumber away to disgorge themselves, and then return for more.

One, two, three . . . eleven, twelve, thirteen — still these yellow monsters come and go, each gaining its fill and bearing it away, though every journey they make, every load they carry, lessens the duration of their reign and hastens the dawn of the new era of the air at Idlewild. One, two, three . . . eleven, twelve, thirteen—mark them as they pass, and many more, and you will see on each a name . . . LeTourneau.

·   ·   ·   ·   ·

Practically to the day that work began at Idlewild another great task was commenced in the cold regions of the North—the construction of the Alaskan Highway.

Stretching through Canadian territory from Dawson Creek to Fairbanks, this strategic road has been claimed as the greatest engineering feat in the history of the

United States Army. Eight miles a day the work went forward—a conquest of men and machines over rain, ice, swamps, rivers, forests, mountains, and a country which has been described as "probably the most forbidding in the world".

An eye-witness* of this epic struggle and achievement has written: "It is the machines that I remember best. . . . The battalion of tractors was like an armored spearhead, which tore open the wilderness for the road. . . . They knocked down the trees, charging them like tanks. These heavy machines were followed by thirty to forty lighter bulldozers and graders. A road-building panzer unit such as this was able to clear a hundred-foot strip through the bush at the rate of four to five miles a day. And there were at least six of these panzer units operating at one time."

Begun in March, 1942, the Alaskan Highway was in service before the close of November of the same year. The great date was October 25, when two parties of military engineers working from opposite directions joined forces, thus completing the last lap of the pioneer road. The honors of the day went to two men who grasped hands across the blades of their bulldozers—yellow monsters we have met before, bearing letters which spell . . . LeTourneau.

.   .   .   .   .   .

June 6, 1944 . . . D-Day! The final chapter of the progress of the war in Europe is opened, as the combined might of Britain and America strikes on the Normandy coast. Men who have trained long and ardu-

---

* Peter Stursberg in *Journey into Victory*.

ously for this moment are there, splendidly equipped and armed.   And prominent among the mechanized accessories of war are mighty machines which have a familiar look.   We have seen their like already.   They are inscribed with a name . . . LeTourneau.

When the first Allied fighter plane landed in Normandy after D-Day military photographers were there to record the event.   The air-strip was scarcely finished when the landing was made; and the developed negative showed the plane almost hidden behind a giant frame bearing the word . . . LeTourneau.   In spite of its bulk it had got there first, and by its labors had prepared the ground for the arrival of the airman.

Earth-moving mammoths!   We have seen them on Long Island's sands preparing the greatest airport the world has yet seen.   We have turned back the clock to describe their contribution to the construction of the Alaskan Road, and the part they played in the war against totalitarian tyranny.   And had we time we might see them still—in California where roads are carved through mountainsides, in West Virginia where black diamonds are being snatched from the bosom of Mother Earth, in Mississippi where levees are being raised to restrain Old Man River . . . and not alone in America, but in Europe, the Orient, the Antipodes, wherever men need strong help to accomplish mighty tasks.

And on every one of these yellow behemoths you may read a name . . . LeTourneau.   Spare me of your time and I will tell you about that name and about the man who bears it.   The story, I promise you, will repay the hearing.

CHAPTER I

A VERMONT FARMHOUSE

I T WAS toward the end of a New England summer, and although the days were still hot and the sun had little pity for those who worked in the fields, the evenings brought welcome relief. After a day's toil on the land it was good to cool off in the comfort of an old familiar chair with a trusted friend beside you to talk over the achievements of the day now ending, and the program of the day that was to come. That, at least, was what Caleb LeTourneau thought, as he kicked his boots from his feet and stretched his tired limbs.

Perched precariously upon the wooden rail which ran the whole length of the farmhouse porch was his friend, Bob Gilmour, wearing an expression on his face which Caleb said he could "read like a book"— an expression which meant that he had something of importance to say.

"What's on your mind, Bob?" Caleb asked, deftly tossing one of Elizabeth's freshly-baked cookies to his companion, who caught it without for a moment upsetting his balance.

"Frankly, Caleb, *you* are on my mind. I've been watching you this summer, and although you have tried to conceal it, I can tell that you are not happy with this farming. I know how you feel about this house and the mill. It was your father's, and he had visions first of Joshua and then of you making a success of it, and extending the property, until the name of LeTourneau would count for something in the Green Mountains. But you know as well as I know that your heart is in other things; things which you cannot hope to do here in Richford . . . "

Caleb rose from his chair, and walked in his stockinged feet to the end of the porch, where he rested his back against the corner post, and half sitting on the rail, looked out across the harvested fields to where The Pinnacle marked the beginning of Canadian territory. And as he did so, his mind began to work backwards through the story of those whose name he bore, Jean and Marie Louise LeTourneau, whose settlement in Richford, Vermont, had been the final chapter in a record of adventure, vicissitude and endurance.

It was to the South of France that memory transported Caleb LeTourneau, and to the city of Lyons, where a small Huguenot community maintained their spiritual integrity against the pressure of fanatical opinion, always threatening to express itself in open persecution. In the flames of religious zeal, fanned by the winds of intolerance, spirits of steel were tempered in men and women who knew no fear except the fear of God, and through whose dispersal the life-blood of many nations was to be enriched.

Jean LeTourneau belonged to this worthy band,

Grandfather of all LeTourneau scrapers, "The Gondola," built in 1922. Primitive compared with present models, it nevertheless made history by being electrically operated and, of course, all-welded.

Contrasted with the previous picture is this Tournapull Carryall with a capacity of 35 tons and a speed of 15 miles per hour. Great machines such as this have revolutionized earth-moving and made the name of LeTourneau famous throughout the world.

Members of the LeTourneau earth-moving family ready for the job. Latest models of bulldozers and scrapers line up at the factory door to be shipped to all parts of the world.

and lagged nowhere behind the rest in conviction or in courage. The faith which he tenaciously held he boldly preached, to the joy and blessing of those who shared his beliefs, and to the confusion of their adversaries. With his finer qualities was an admixture of impulsiveness and reckless resolve, which, if it sometimes threatened to bring him into trouble, was nevertheless a spur to high endeavor.

As Jean preached, so he wooed, with intensity and ardor; and Marie Louise, the woman of his choice, returned his love in generous measure. In spite of the objections of her parents, who considered Jean too poor for one who had been born with the advantages of wealth, she wedded the preacher. Whether this defiance of the parental ban contributed to the early departure of the young couple from the scenes of their childhood cannot be known; but, whatever the reason, before long Jean and Marie Louise took farewell of their native France, and made the then hazardous crossing of the Atlantic to settle in Quebec.

Associating himself in Canada with men and women who shared his views, Jean became a teacher in the Grand Ligne Mission, and continued to preach. But soon ill-health made it necessary for him to turn his eyes toward the South in search of a more congenial climate. Thus the decision was made to exchange Canada for the United States, and Jean brought his wife to live in Richford, Vermont, among whose people he found kindred spirits, many of whom had come from France by the same route that he had travelled.

To this day, the largest foreign element in Vermont is composed of French-Canadian farmers.

For a time, Jean LeTourneau maintained a boarding-school in Richford, but his health did not improve, and the choice of an outdoor life became imperative. A farmhouse and a mill were acquired a little north of the town—the very same house in whose porch Jean's son, Caleb, now sat talking with Bob Gilmour, his friend.

Caleb recalled all this, as he gazed northward toward the frontier. It was an apparent accident that he had succeeded to the farm, as Bob Gilmour had hinted. Jean had intended that Joshua should be the farmer, and Caleb the man of letters; but by the loss of an arm Joshua incapacitated himself for heavy manual work, so the plan had been reversed. Joshua should now wield the pen, and Caleb the plough.

Had it been right or wrong to change the direction of two lives on account of a seemingly fortuitous occurrence? Caleb had often asked the question—had, indeed, argued it out point by point with Bob. And it was with complete understanding of his friend's attitude toward the farm and its responsibilities that Bob had again broached the subject of removal to another part of the country, where among pioneering communities he and Caleb might make a fresh start in tasks chosen by themselves, and not dictated to them by others.

"Bob," said Caleb at last, taking his friend by the arm, and walking with him toward the porch steps, "you're right. If it hadn't been for Elizabeth and the children I guess you and I would have gone long ago. But it's no good putting this off indefinitely. We aren't getting younger, and opportunities are slipping by. We'll see this winter through, Bob, for more reasons than one; and then, old friend, you and I will do a little prospecting together."

Caleb watched Bob disappear into the distance, and then turned and entered the house. Elizabeth was busy. That was no matter for surprise, for she was never anything else. Caleb had good reason to remember the approval given by Bob Gilmour to his choice of a partner—"A girl that's up every morning at four to do the chores'll make a good match for you." So, indeed, it had turned out; and now, with three little ones to care for and a fourth expected, Elizabeth's days were fuller than ever. But her responsibilities were cheerfully borne, and at the end of a heavy day in the fields her husband could always depend upon a loving welcome when he returned home.

"Harold 'n Willie 'n Mattie?" enquired Caleb, after kissing his wife.

"In bed. I would have sent them out to say good-night if you and Bob hadn't been so busily talking. There's no need to ask the subject, Caleb. What does Bob want to do now?"

"He wants to go West, Liz, and maybe South, too. But he doesn't want to go more than I do. We've talked about this long enough, and talking isn't getting us anywhere. I guess we'll have to do something, and do it pretty quick. If we let time slip by any more it will soon be too late. It's now or never."

Caleb had seated himself at the table for the meal which Elizabeth had spread for him there, and she spared herself a moment to sit beside him.

"I know how you and Bob feel," she said, "and I guess you're right. Farming's just hard work for you, Caleb, and all the harder because you don't really like it. Out West you could build, and then you'd be happy. There's hundreds of folk trekking westward, and all of them want homes. And there'll be stables and barns and stores, too, all to be put up. I'm sure there's a living for us in the West . . . but you wouldn't be going just yet?"

There were those who thought Caleb LeTourneau a rough man, and the severity of his expression sometimes lent color to that supposition. But those who thus judged him would have been surprised if they could have seen him at that moment, as he pressed Elizabeth's hand to his lips, and looked lovingly into her eyes.

"No, not just yet, Liz," he reassured her. "I told Bob that we couldn't go this side of the winter. And though he said nothing, I'm sure he understood."

"He understood all right," smiled Elizabeth, rising to remove the dishes. "Why, Bob's as excited as we are over the new baby. And why shouldn't he be, since you have promised him that if he's a boy he shall be named after him. Robert Gilmour LeTourneau! It sounds good to me, Caleb; and although in this matter you didn't consult me, I guess it'll do."

.   .   .   .

It *was* a boy who came to the LeTourneau farm-house on November 30, 1888, and in fulfilment of the promise he received the name of his father's friend. The town clerk of Richford tried to deprive Bob Gilmour of the full glory of that bestowment by two errors in the official registry of births, by the first of which he omitted the distinctive name of Gilmour, and by the second mispelled the French patronymic. "Lestourneau, Robert," was the entry which stood uncorrected until 1943, when, through the industrious inquiries and representations of Clifton Brannon, attorney to the R. G. LeTourneau Company of Texas, the clerk's blunders were atoned for by a fresh entry, which reads: "LeTourneau, Robert Gilmour, son of Caleb Thucydides LeTourneau and Elizabeth Johnson LeTourneau."

CHAPTER II

YOUNG ROBERT

WHEN Caleb and Bob went West they followed the route of the covered wagons but enjoyed the convenience of the railroad, which was good for their wives, who were awaiting their return, eager to know how far they and the children must travel to their new homes.

It was here that Brother Joshua stepped in, and by his intervention curbed the enthusiasm of the two friends, and thus reduced the mileage which the woman and children had to cover. For Caleb and Bob had proceeded from the Pacific Coast into Lower California, Mexico, where they actually bought a piece of land. But on their way home they stopped at Duluth, Minnesota, to call on Joshua, who was editor of a newspaper in that city.

Joshua wanted a house built, and he had high regard for Caleb as a builder. So, with all the skill of a journalist, he described the advantages of Duluth as a place of residence and of business. Why go further, when that growing city offered all the opportunity a man could desire? Duluth needed a good building contractor—and Caleb was that—so why not settle there? How successful were Joshua's persuasions is demonstrated by the fact that, in spite of the land pur-

22

chase in Lower California, when Caleb and Bob moved from Richford it was to Duluth they went.

The transfer was made in easy stages, mainly in the interests of Elizabeth and the children. First of all Caleb sold the farm. Then he took his wife and the family to her father's home at Beebe Plains. And finally, when all was conveniently arranged, he left for Duluth alone, purposing to build a home for himself first, and next one for Joshua, and after that for anybody who sought his services and paid his price.

And now that the farmhouse has been vacated, and the little family is on the move toward the West, it is time to consider a little more closely the subject of our story—young Robert Gilmour LeTourneau, aged one-and-a-half, and rapidly growing. Adjectives are so prodigally used to describe children that a self-imposed restraint is necessary to guard against excess of zeal. Truth to tell, the infant R. G. revealed none of those qualities which constitute a prodigy; a fact which is enthusiastically recorded since few of the abnormalities of human achievement and development are more objectionable than boy marvels.

Nevertheless, Caleb and Elizabeth must often have wondered what sort of a child this was that had come to occupy the fourth place in their still growing family. Certainly none of the three who preceded him, or of the four who followed, was cast in the same mold of self-will. As a small baby he objected to staying in bed, and expressed his objection in untiring efforts to get up no matter how often he was laid upon the pillow. Elizabeth, tender-hearted mother though she was, realized that in this battle of wills there could be no quarter, for the good of the child himself. So there was one occasion when the struggle was prolonged for two hours, until the little body was wearied and sleep was induced. That particular fight was never again refought, though once, when some infantile malady demanded the administration of medicine, two-year-old Robert resisted the proffered dose for so long and with such physical energy that at length he sank limply upon the bed, exhausted by his expenditure of strength. In later years his mother recalled with amusement how frightened she was until, his customary vim restored, the beloved adversary resumed the struggle.

The relations between mother and child, however, were not always combative, for, like his brothers and sisters, Robert learned to love Elizabeth's sweet voice and gentle manner, often so sharply in contrast with her husband's severity. She had one particularly delightful aptitude: as life's varied pattern unfolded before her children, she was always ready with a rhyme to match the new experience. Where she obtained all those jingles and verses which charmed the youthful ears is impossible to say; of some she must herself have been the composer. And in years to come, when glad reunions brought the family together—Harold, William, Mattie, Robert, Sarah, Marie, Philip and Louis—sooner or later somebody was bound to refer to Mother's rhymes, and privileged listeners were amazed to find how deep was the impression they had made, so deep that time could not erase the memory.

But to return to Robert. The trail of his boyhood years was littered with toys deliberately pulled to pieces "to see how they work", with watches and clocks ruined for ever because of his inquisitive mind, with strange contraptions of wood and metal in which he strove to express some idea that was burning in his brain. But these are the performances of normal boyhood, and cannot legitimately be claimed as the early manifestations of genius.

Two traits only obtrude from his childhood: that adamantine will to which we have already referred, and an incurable restlessness of body and of mind. Sister Marie tells how, when he could scarcely toddle, he disturbed the peace of the house by beating his feet on the floor, chanting monotonously as he did so: "I want *something* to do! I want *something* to do! I want *something* to do!" "And there was no stopping him," she adds, "until Mother found something for him to do."

With all his drive, however—and maybe because of it—young Robert did not take kindly to school. Sitting still was purgatory to him, for it was unproductive. Only once, so the rest of the family declared, had he remained on a chair for more than five minutes, and that was when an unsuspecting visitor, himself disturbed by the boy's fidgetiness, had offered him a nickel to sit still for that length of time. Robert had carried out his part of the bargain with his eye on the coming payment; and at the end of the five minutes announced that he was ready to repeat the performance for another nickel.

It might be kindness to pass over the school years with a minimum of comment. The educational pundits of the world have not yet learned how to adapt their rigid curriculums to children who take more kindly to a hammer and chisel, or a canvas and brush, or a music score and a piano than they do to logarithms and Latin; so it was not to be wondered at that this small bundle of energy and ideas which bore the name of Robert Gilmour LeTourneau should be an academic misfit.

Father Caleb, who always lamented the meagreness of his own education, and coveted learning for his boys and girls, was distressed over this lack of progress; but distress turned to dismay when Robert was fired from his first job. He was about thirteen, and the time had come when he should take over the newspaper round which had been satisfactorily worked first by Brother Harold and then by Brother Bill. There was not much to it: the newspapers were clearly marked, and all that was necessary was to deposit them in the appropriate porches, well out of the rain or the snow. Easy? Of course it was; too easy, in fact, for Robert, who found it impossible to concentrate upon a task so simple and automatic. Before long, complaints were lodged with the news-agent that papers had not been delivered, or that they were being left in the wrong porch. Robert was admonished, but failed to reform. As he walked his morning round he was too busy building a world of fancy all his own to bother with the *Courier* or the *Herald,* and the houses to which they belonged. So Robert and the job parted company, leaving the former poorer by twelve cents a day.

If that twelve cents had been going into his own pocket, Robert would doubtless have been more concerned to retain the newspaper round; but it had been earmarked for the family purse. When Caleb heard the news, he sent for his unemployed son, gravely rebuked him for the disgrace he had brought upon himself ("Harold and Bill worked well, and kept the round open for you, and now you've lost it!"), impressed upon him the serious financial loss that was involved for the family (actually things were very comfortable in the LeTourneau home, and the daily twelve cents was only extorted as a matter of training and discipline), and then announced:

"You'll make up for that twelve cents, my boy, by cutting wood every morning."

"How much wood?" inquired Robert, anxious to know the extent of his obligation.

"Twelve cents' worth, of course," came the answer, with this additional information, which proved that with all his apparent severity Caleb knew the mentality of the lad he was handling—"And for every stick you cut beyond that I'll pay you a cent for your own pocket."

"I bought myself my first rifle out of that deal," R. G. will tell you today, with keen satisfaction over the way in which he abandoned the non-lucrative paper round for a more congenial task which benefited the household and paid him well into the bargain.

As may be gathered, Robert liked cutting wood, and his zeal in this was responsible for an incident with his father which brought to a crisis the strained relations between them. For Caleb found it very difficult to exercise patience toward his overgrown son, who had the body of a man, the strength of a horse, and—as he sometimes allowed himself to think—the obstinacy of a demon.

Like George Washington, our Robert caused the trouble with a hatchet. Wood was wanted for the hearth, and with characteristic impetuousness he seized the first timber he could find, and setting to, soon had it cut into convenient lengths. Later that day, Caleb discovered that some prized palings were missing, and the awful truth was revealed that young Bob had cut them up for firewood.

What the father said in his anger is best forgotten, even as it would have been better unsaid; for Caleb had a fiery temper and a searing tongue, for both of which he constantly sought the forgiveness of God and of men. The hasty, unmeasured words he used that day injured the spirit of the offending boy. "Father has neither love nor use for me," he said to himself, ruminating upon earlier occasions when he had been sternly rebuked, and had planned to run away. This time, he carried that resolve into effect. He left home.

The speedy approach of Christmas set a problem

for the exiled youth. He knew that, as for many Christmases past, the entire family would be gathering at Uncle 'Manuel's, when everybody would ask: "Where's Bob?" In his imagination he could see his mother's face as she winced under the inquiry, and sought for a reply which would not abuse the truth and yet conceal the facts. There was only one thing he could do to spare her the ordeal; he must put his pride in his pocket, and present himself with the rest.

He felt a bit of a fraud that Christmas Day, as he tried to behave normally, and he was not a little grateful to the other members of the family for preserving his secret. On the whole, the day passed happily; but when the time to disperse came round a blizzard raging outside made it necessary for the women and children to spend the night under Uncle 'Manuel's roof, while the men and youths fought their way home.

In these unexpected circumstances, therefore, Robert found himself in the company of his father in a two-mile walk through heavy snow and wind. Somehow or other, the very fierceness of the weather seemed to draw the little band together in friendliness which obliterated the past; and when the LeTourneau home was reached, it was Caleb himself who suggested that Robert should not continue the journey to his lodging, but turn in with the rest for the night. Next morning, Robert had to stay for breakfast. Then, when the others began cutting wood, he felt obliged to lend them a hand. And so it was soon dinner time, and they sat down together to a hearty meal, at which Robert was now a willing guest. After eating, he was under an even heavier obligation to help his father and four brothers. Thus the day passed, every hour drawing father and son closer together.

"That day I got to know my father as I had never known him before," was Robert's subsequent testimony, "and I began to realize what difficulty he had faced with a wistful, stubborn boy. From that time onward we were the best of friends."

CHAPTER III

THE "ONE TOOL" MECHANIC

WHEN Robert was fourteen he announced that he wanted to leave school, and neither his parents nor his teachers could find a good reason to refuse his request. That method of instruction which puts a boy to a desk for long hours each day had never agreed with him, and there was reason to believe that no extension of his school days would add materially to his meagre store of academic knowledge. He was not, however, without equipment for the battle of life, for if he had profited little from class instruction, he had nevertheless learned how to do things with his hands. So the boy's formal education was ended, and he began a new chapter in his life in which he was to prove himself an apter pupil than most in the school of experience.

Just about this time, the family moved from Duluth to Portland, Oregon, and there Robert obtained employment in an iron foundry. It was heavy work, but he enjoyed it, and considered himself fortunate to be away from copy-books and primers. "I would rather pound iron twelve hours a day than go to school," he answered one person who inquired whether he was not sorry to have begun work so soon.

Although destruction by fire of the iron foundry

in Portland terminated his apprenticeship there, Robert sought the continuation of his training elsewhere, and emerged a competent master-moulder, with a keen practical interest in the qualities of metals and their constructional possibilities. He delighted in fashioning this tough, durable material until it yielded to his wishes and expressed his ideas—and already his mind was filled with visions of the machines which he would one day create.

Apparent misfortune was responsible for placing in his hands a tool which was to become the symbol of his enterprise. He had been on the pay-roll of an iron foundry in Oakland, and was laid off with other men. Not wishing to be idle, he looked around for a suitable opening, and noticed a group of men working in the yard of a power station. Clearly, there was enough work on hand there to justify an increase in staff; so Robert presented himself as an applicant for a job. He was accepted, and sent to assist one of the lead-burners—men whose task it was to clean up and repair the plates of the large storage batteries. For this purpose a welding torch was used.

It was the newcomer's responsibility to prepare the plates for the operator, and this Robert did with efficiency. But when the other man got to work with his torch he never took his eyes off him. That particular tool fascinated him. It was a man's tool, an artist's tool, and as its superheated flame made the metal flow, young Robert came to believe that there was nothing it could not do.

He was the happiest fellow on earth that day when his workmate first placed the welding-torch in his hand, and showed him how to use it. After that, he gave him many opportunities to gain experience, and these were gratefully seized and used to good advantage. After a few weeks of practice in this way, Robert found himself alone in the room, and resolved to prove himself as good a lead-burner as the other. With intense application he directed the flame along the plate, manipulating it with surprising skill, and gaining great satisfaction as he saw the results. So engrossed was he that he failed to notice somebody enter the room and stand behind him. When at last he did look up, there was . . . the big boss.

"I guess I'll have to get you a torch."

That was all the big boss said, but it was music in Robert's ears; and he realized that he had made a real step forward when from that day he was rated as a qualified lead-burner. The time was to come when he would be known as the "one-tool mechanic". "Bob's crazy," people said. "He welds everything!" It was even rumored that he welded the buttons to his trousers. But with unruffled confidence in the possibilities of the welding process he kept on his way, ignoring experts and ignoramuses alike, and refusing to be influenced by any opinion so long as his process stood the test of "Will it work?"

Among the many surprising contraptions which he produced was an automobile rigged up as a mobile welding shop. Doubtless it looked weird and wonderful; but what did appearance matter if the thing did its job? One day, a neighbor got in trouble with his ditching machine. Could Bob send out his welding plant and mend it? Bob took on the commission, and having a man in his employ, sent him out to make the necessary repairs.

So satisfactory was the result that the neighbor began to think of other pieces of equipment which were lying idle for want of repair. Could the welding plant be sent to his yard to fix these? Bob was only too willing; and for three days the torch that melted and mended was busy—and all the time earning good money for its proprietor. In fact, at the end of the three days the neighbor woke up to the fact that he was running up a considerable bill with Robert Gilmour LeTourneau. "If your machine stays here any longer," he said, "it will be paid for—*but it won't be mine!*" Its owner chuckled—as he was often to chuckle in the years that followed when his "crazy" ideas brought in the dollars. "Why not have one of your own?" he suggested. And the neighbor, thinking that an excellent scheme, ordered a duplicate of the mobile welder for his own use— and paid more good hard cash when it was delivered.

After a brief interval at farming, during which he demonstrated that he had a great capacity for absorbing knowledge by successfully mastering a series of correspondence courses in mathematics and engineering, Robert turned his attention to automobile repairs —an interest that was awakened by the possession of a motor-cycle. For a while he worked for an employer, but it was not long before he and another young man decided to go into business for themselves. Things went well with them, for there was not much that the partner did not know about trading and accounts, while Robert's reputation as a repair mechanic brought in as many jobs as they could handle.

Thus engaged, he found more and more uses for his welding torch. By now, of course, he was using a much more efficient tool than the one which he first handled at Oakland, for the oxyacetylene method was now generally employed, and he had taken care to learn all about it from the start. So, from joining broken parts of cars and reuniting chassis joints he progressed to more ambitious uses for his favorite tool, and began to construct his own equipment from pieces of steel which he was able to purchase at a considerable saving.

The garage partnership at Stockton, California, continued satisfactorily until 1917, when the entry of the United States into the First World War challenged Robert with a patriotic duty which he answered by offering his services at the Navy Yard, Vallejo, California. When he first presented himself he boldly filled in a form asking for engagement as a welder. But the interviewing official glanced at the entry, and shook his head. There were no vacancies for welders. That was a disappointment, but he was determined to press his application, so he asked for a second blank. On this, he described himself as an electrician: but the response was the same. There were no vacancies for electricians.

Robert scratched his head in momentary perplexity, and then, requesting a third form, he presented himself afresh as a machinist. But no machinists were wanted, and his demand for yet another form was met by the discouraging advice: "You'd better go home, fellow." Obviously, the official did not know his man. Robert was not being put off as easily as that, and he insisted that there must be something in the Navy Yard that he could do. At last, his persistence brought reward; and the "one-tool mechanic" was signed on as a second-class welder.

What aggravation of spirit he endured during the weeks that followed can only be left to the imagination. The "first-class" welders whom he had to assist scarcely knew one end of a torch from the other; and the quality of their work almost made him cry out in disgust. It was such a trial of patience for him that he determined to obtain a transfer to some other part of the yard as soon as he could, and with this in mind he kept his eyes open for possible alternatives.

One day, he discovered that there was an electrical machine-shop where he could be happily and profitably employed. Now the question was: How could he obtain the necessary transfer? He laid in wait for the shop superintendent, gained his ear while he told his story, and managed to persuade him that he would be a useful man. "I'll take you, if you can get release from your present foreman," he promised.

To obtain such permission was the real difficulty,

but Robert set about it with his usual determination. He thought up all the possible reasons why he should be transferred from welding to the electrical machine-shop, and poured them into the foreman's ear. But that man wasn't interested. Maybe he wanted to keep a hand who could make circles round the majority of his welders. So he tried to ignore Robert, which, of course, only made him more insistent. Robert talked on and on until, in the spirit of the judge toward the importunate widow, the foreman exclaimed: "Oh, all right, you can go!"

This grudging consent was forthwith reported to the superintendent of the machine-shop, but to Robert's disappointment he replied that he must have it in writing. This meant a return to the welding foreman, who by now repented his earlier action, and declared that he had given no consent. So once again the battle was joined, until at last the foreman, wearied by the argument, gave the requisite formal notice, and Robert was transferred to a job in which he gained experience that was to be invaluable in the years to come. He had been refused employment as an electrician. He had likewise been refused as a machinist. But as an electrical-machinist he was now put to work.

The shop superintendent had been impressed by Robert's eagerness and display of knowledge, and naturally assumed that the new hand was fully experienced. The fact was, however, that he knew very little about actual operation of machines, and before long he found himself up against the problem of being in charge of equipment which he did not know how to use. He surveyed the machine from end to end, but could not even tell for sure how the thing was started.

Had this occurred a few weeks earlier, he would have been in a real predicament, for some of the other men had not taken kindly to the newcomer, and were not disposed to help him. But it had been discovered that he was a motor mechanic, and a fellow employee with an automobile that wouldn't go had gratefully accepted his help; and with his car once more on the road, and running better than it had ever gone before, he sung the praises of the aspiring electrician. That brought plenty of other customers, whose cars he fixed at the end of each working day.

So now he had friends enough, and to one of these he went with his dilemma. It would not do to display his ignorance for all to see, so they went together to another shop where a similar machine was installed; and there, in a few minutes, all the instruction necessary was given. Robert returned to his own shop, threw over the lever, and was soon feeding and tending his machine as though he had been doing it all his life.

At the end of the war, Robert returned to Stockton and the garage. But there an unpleasant surprise awaited him. In his absence, the partner had piled up debts and ruined a good business through insobriety and extravagance. An effort to straighten things out, which lasted for six months, proved unavailing. Robert decided to quit the garage business, and to find other means of earning money, whereby he could discharge his proportion of a debt of $5,000.

"What are you going to do now, Bob?" asked a friend, meeting him upon the street.

"Take the first job that comes along," was the answer.

Then and there he learned of a proposition which was after his heart. A rancher in the neighborhood wanted a man to overhaul some tractors and keep them in good repair; but he required some evidence of ability, and suggested that whoever became responsible for his tractors should first repair a boat engine which by general verdict had seen its last days. Robert asked to see the boat engine, got busy on it, soon had it in running order, and was forthwith appointed Tractor-Engineer-in-Chief.

To mention at this point that Robert was now a married man may seem to pay scant regard to the importance of his marriage or to the lady who had become his wife. But if the reader will have patience, the full story of Robert's wooing and winning of Evelyn Peterson will be related in due time, and placed at the very heart of our record—which, indeed, is the place where it belongs. Let it suffice to say now, therefore, that he was two years married when he gave up the garage business, that he was still very much in love (though not less than Evelyn), and that the one flaw in his new job in the San Joaquin Valley was that it involved temporary separation. But Evelyn was as determined as Robert to liquidate the debt, and she made her own contribution by accepting employment as nursemaid to a family in the same neighborhood.

For the newly-weds, however, it was a case of "so near and yet so far". Between the farm where Robert wrestled with his tractors and the house where Evelyn nursed her babies there was a deep, fast-running stream. And there was no bridge by which to cross it. Love, however, is not cheated by little things like that; and Robert kept regular tryst with his dear one by building a raft, on which he placed his clothes after undressing on the near bank of the river, then swimming across with the raft pushed before him, so that he could dress on the opposite bank, and present himself properly attired before his wife.

It wasn't the best arrangement, of course, but it produced much-needed money, and it was endured in the knowledge that it would not last forever. Robert was very satisfied with his work, which brought good remuneration, and enabled him to save, while Evelyn added to her treasure chest every week a few dollars toward the thousands that had to be repaid.

So six months went by, and then something happened which was unexceptional enough to excite no immediate interest, but which, if it could have been seen in the light of what was to follow, would have been recognized as the turning-point of a life.

"There's a piece of land over there that I want levelled. Would you do it for me?" Robert was interested in his employer's suggestion. Looking after machines had been good fun, but making them do things was even more to his liking, and he thrilled to the task as he took over an old tractor and scraper and turned them loose upon the field in which he was to iron out the bumps and fill in the hollows, and produce land which would be ready for sowing with alfalfa.

It was a ramshackle combination which, with the help of another man, he directed back and forth, shaving off a few feet of earth here, filling in again there, and leaving behind a creditably level strip of ever-growing dimensions. But as they banged and clattered and hissed their way along, Robert's brain was hard at work. The blade of the scraper was operated by compressed air, and required the attention of one man, while the other drove the tractor. It was not a happy combination, for sooner or later the two men would fail to synchronize their actions, and the trouble which ensued would involve an explosion of tempers, apart from the possible damage to the machines. Then, instead of scraping earth, the operators might turn to scraping the skin off one another's noses.

Now, if only the tractor-driver could also have control of the scraper; if only, from his driving seat, he could operate the steel blade which changed the contours of the land; if only ... if only ...

Yes, Robert had it! He was sure that the thing could be done by substituting electrical power for compressed air; and from then onward, when not engaged in the actual task of land-levelling, he was working on the great-grandfather of all LeTourneau earthmoving machines: a scraper which economized in manpower, since it required the services of one operator instead of two, and therefore saved time, for a committee of one can always be trusted to get things done with the utmost expedition.

The substitution of electricity for compressed air not only pleased Robert, but also the man for whom he worked. So much so that when Robert decided that the land-levelling business had possibilities which he would like to pursue on his own, and accordingly gave notice to the rancher and proceeded to remove his electrical gadgets from the scraper so as to restore it to its original condition, the owner called a halt. "I'll buy that gear from you," he proposed, "and you can build another for yourself."

Do you recall Robert's mobile welding plant? Then you will remember that the man for whom it was operated was so convinced of its usefulness that he wanted it for himself, and paid Robert to build him one. And do you notice that precisely the same thing was happening again? Here was our young inventor planning to go into land-levelling as a contractor, but before he could make a start at that he was being thrust into the business of manufacturer. And that's how it was for many years that followed, until at last the manufacturer crowded the contractor out, and instead of operating machines Robert concentrated his genius on the designing and production of machines for others to operate.

But we are progressing a little too fast, for we have yet to get Robert promoted as a contractor. To do this he had to raise the price of a tractor and scraper that would be his very own. He had little difficulty in enlisting the help of a banker acquaintance, and so, in the year 1920, we find him the proud possessor of a 75 Holt tractor, with all the gear that was necessary to level land. His reputation as an earth-mover was in process of being built.

It was to be expected that he would not be satisfied for long with apparatus that was the product of somebody else's brain. He soon saw faults in the scraper, and figured out ways in which it could be improved. One thing he particularly disliked—the whole job was riveted, and he took that as a reflection upon the potentialities of his welding-torch. He was convinced that welding was a better process than riveting—provided, of course, that it was good welding. So, just to prove his point, he bought some steel, lit up his acetylene torch, and got to work.

Once again, somebody saw his product, liked it, wanted one for himself, and asked Robert to build it. And the second all-welded scraper was in many respects better than the first, for, as the whole world now

knows, LeTourneau never stands still. If he designs
a machine, and it is satisfactory, he is not happy until
by some improvement he makes it more so. And should
he design a machine that is not satisfactory (Hush!
even that has been known to happen!), then out on the
scrap-heap it goes, and R. G. starts all over again until
he has produced something which passes his critical
judgment.

(You will note our introduction of those initials—
R. G.   They are deliberately used at this point, since
Robert is now about to become the Man of Big Business, an employer of others, a figure in the industrial
world, and as R. G. he is to gain a position of authority
and success which those who knew Robert would never
have suspected. So, from now on, it shall mainly be
as R. G. that he features in this story; though we may
be allowed latitude to call him Mr. LeTourneau if we
so choose, or even plain Bob, which is probably the
name that he prefers.   But mostly it shall be—R. G.)

Very well, then, meet R. G. LeTourneau, Land-
Levelling Contractor!

It was during this period of his life that R. G. made
two contacts which are of exceptional interest, and
proved of great value in later years.   The first was
with a lawyer named Carlton C. Case.   R. G. contracted to level land for this lawyer, and while doing
so learned of his intention to install a concrete pipe for
irrigation purposes.   The nearest place where concrete
piping was made was twenty miles away, which meant
heavy costs for haulage.   R. G. had ideas of his own

about the construction of concrete piping, so he passed them on to Mr. Case, with the suggestion that, instead of purchasing his requirements, he should make them on the spot. "Very well, then," the lawyer came back, "what about you doing it for me?"

So, as a diversion from land-levelling, R. G. tried his hand at pipeline manufacture; and foot by foot the pipe was made and laid. It looked a fine job, and everyone was pleased with it, until the water was turned on, when the pipe was found to leak at every joint. Not for the last time in his life, R. G. was learning by making mistakes.

Unfortunately, he had been paid progress money by Mr. Case, which placed him in the embarrassing position of having received payment for unsatisfactory work. That was a matter demanding rectification, and R. G. resolved that, however long it took and however much it cost, the pipeline would be put right. So he put himself to school to discover where he had gone wrong, and he did it by watching the manufacture of concrete piping, and standing by as an observant spectator while it was being laid.

While he was doing this, the astute lawyer, fearing that the explanation of the trouble was that his contractor had tried to economize on costs to his own advantage by using too little cement in the mixture, took a length of the faulty pipe to an analyst, and awaited the report. When it came through it proved that R. G. had been unusually generous in his use of cement, so that, in this respect, Carlton Case was getting full value for his money.

In ignorance of this investigation and its results, R. G. returned from his mission of inquiry, and proceeded to put into effect what he had learned. Using an effective agent, he sealed the leaky joints with his own hands, spending hours each day on his knees. It took him a month to finish the task, but the time was well spent, for it won him a true and lasting friend in Carlton Case, who became his adviser and attorney, remaining so until the day of his death.

The other contact was with a paving contractor out West. R. G. had sold him some earth-moving machines, which worked so well that, being a Big Man with a big vision, he suggested he should buy out R. G. LeTourneau and add him and his staff to his own pay-roll. (To this episode we shall return on a later page.) This arrangement held for six months, but even after it had ended, the two men remained in close association.

One day, the paving contractor saw a new dump-wagon which R. G. had designed for his own use, and recognized its possibilities for a big job which he had in hand, building levees along the Mississippi River. He accordingly ordered a number of the wagons. In the process of manufacture, R. G. slightly modified the design, believing that he could improve on the original model. When it came to a demonstration, however, the designer himself realized that he had made a mistake, and that the revised design would not be one-hundred per cent efficient for transporting the wet soil of the Mississippi banks. He confessed as much to his customer; but the Big Man did not share that view, and declared himself altogether satisfied with the wagons.

It was a little annoying, therefore, after the wagons had been finished and delivered, that R. G. should receive a complaint that they were not giving good service, coupled with the request that he should personally inspect them in operation. Time was valuable just then, and feeling that the contractor himself was to blame for what had occurred, R. G. sent back the reply that he would go, but on the condition that his expenses were paid. Shortly afterward came the reply that he need not trouble.

R. G. knew that he had made a mistake, and when the Big Man overheated the wires of the telephone as he ventilated his thoughts on the matter, he submitted to the stinging rebuke in the realization that he had asked for it. Before he could express regret in reply, the other man hung up on him. A visit to his customer's office brought no satisfaction; and a subsequent attempt to make amends by personal apology was curtly stifled. It looked as though the parting was final.

Then, one day, R. G. had a telephone call from one of the Big Man's managers. A large crane, engaged in vital work, had broken down, and repairs effected in the normal way would mean the loss of hundreds of thousands of dollars. "*He* believes that you could weld it. Will you come and see?"

This was a situation that needed tactful handling, for the misunderstanding had arisen over a refusal to travel, yet R. G. knew that the better course would be for the engine to be sent to him rather than for him to go to the engine. So, with carefully-chosen words he made his proposal, which was accepted, and the disabled machine was sent by express methods to the Stockton workshop. That night, the small LeTourneau plant was noisy with the cracking of welding-torches, and livid with their incandescent light. All through the hours of darkness proprietor and staff worked on that engine, and early the following day it was back again where it was so urgently needed—and it worked so well that a companion unit was despatched to Stockton to receive identical treatment.

"You haven't sent in your bill for those jobs." Several weeks had passed since that night of fevered activity, and the Big Man's manager was again on the telephone.

"No," came the reply, "and there isn't going to be a bill!"

"No bill! Why not?"

Then to R. G. came the opportunity for which he had been longing and praying.

"You know how things have been between me and the boss. I have been waiting for this day to put things right between us. I know I was wrong over the Mississippi job. I want him to know I am sorry. That's why there will be no bill. So if you can put in a word for me, I'll be more than grateful."

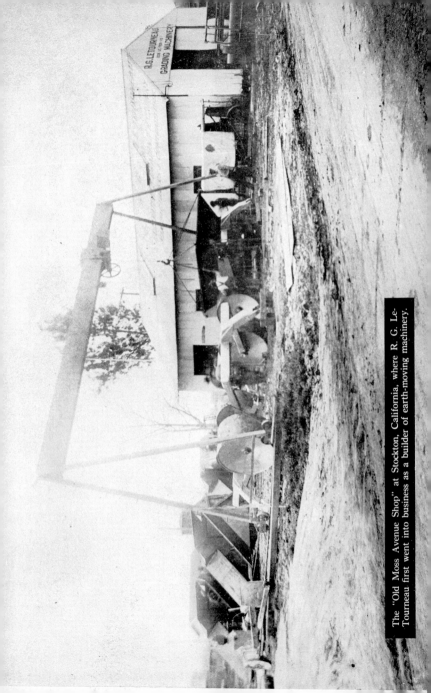

The "Old Moss Avenue Shop" at Stockton, California, where R. G. Le-Tourneau first went into business as a builder of earth-moving machinery.

Big, high-powered engines on the assembly line at the Peoria factory. The largest is rated at 300 h.p., but contractors are always asking for more powerful machines, and Mr. LeTourneau is always ready to " put on more horses."

Time passed, and there was no word from the Big Man. Then one day he called R. G. personally on the 'phone. He was an even Bigger Man now, and was contractor for the concrete piers to the great San Francisco bridge. To keep a personal eye on things, he used a small fast motor-boat, which was his pride and joy. The boat had broken down. "The casing of the engine has fractured. It's a welding job, and only you can fix it, Bob. Will you help me?"

Bob had a heavy week-end before him, with matters of first importance to attend to the following day. But he said, "Yes!" and taking a reliable helper with him, jumped into his car and drove eighty miles to where the boat was anchored. Into the night they worked, and by four o'clock in the morning the casing was repaired. There was no time to lose if the new day's appointment was to be kept, so the car sped back over the eighty miles to Stockton, where, after a necessary scrub down, the journey was resumed to Sunday's rendezvous—a further ninety miles away.

That duty discharged (patience! and you shall know all about it) R. G. returned to the motor-boat, just to make sure that all was well. He found the Big Man delighted. "Jump in, Bob, and I'll show you what she will do." Bob jumped in; and when he tells of that experience today he confesses that what followed was one of the thrills of his life. "He would cut off the engine, almost stopping the boat. Then, suddenly, he would throw her in again so that she literally leapt out of the water and came down again with a thud and a splash. Then he would dart away ploughing deeply into the water, turning and twisting the boat so that it seemed that something must break. And all the time he was laughing like a child in his enjoyment."

Take another look at that man in the boat, for his name is Henry J. Kaiser, prince of manufacturers, builder of Liberty ships in World War II, and present-day challenger of the American automobile market. Are you surprised to find our Robert in such company, and on such intimate terms? Maybe you would have been even more surprised if you could have seen the company he was in on the previous day. For the engagement which he worked all night to keep, adding to his toil a road journey of nearly 200 miles, was a meeting for young people—yes, a religious meeting!

And that, of course, demands an explanation.

Chapter IV

A LIGHT FROM HEAVEN

YOUNG ROBERT revealed some traits of character which were less agreeable than others. Perhaps you have suppressed the thought out of regard for the fact that our subject is still with us, and out of respect for the position which he now holds. If so, away with such restraints, and let us know the worst.

If ever Caleb and Elizabeth imagined that they had produced a cherub in their fourth child, that hallucination was short-lived. Remember the imperious infant of eighteen months who would not stay in bed! By an incredible stubbornness the growing boy endeavored to enforce his will on parents and brothers and sisters alike, and there were tempers and tantrums when his plans went awry. This meant innumerable clashes with Caleb, who saw duplicated in his son his own hasty nature, with this important exception, that it was not as yet curbed by the influence of religion.

Sometimes it seemed to Elizabeth that this headstrong boy must become the black sheep of the family; another sad demonstration of the fact that Christian privilege and example do not necessarily lead to Christian living. His grandfather had been a preacher of the Gospel. Caleb himself was no mean expositor of the Scriptures. And as for Elizabeth, she had once had ambitions for the mission-field, but failing to realize that high calling had accepted motherhood as God's plan for her, declaring that if she could not go as a missionary to the heathen abroad, she would do her best to prevent her children from increasing the number of the heathen at home.

It looked, however, as though her resolve was to fail in the case of Robert. There was no open rejection of God in his life. On the contrary, he knelt with the rest at the family altar, and was to be found at public worship as each Sunday came round. There were, in fact, occasions when under the preaching of the Gospel he showed signs of spiritual concern; but these hopeful indications produced no permanent results, and the noticeable drift of this young life was away from God and righteousness.

By the time he was sixteen, Robert had formed companionships which were highly dangerous, and those who loved him grew more and more concerned over his manner of life. But there was one thing which held out promise of a change; the boy himself was unhappy. Down in his heart he knew that he was sinning against the light, and the conviction grew upon him that if he persisted in his evil course he would be doubly guilty in the sight of God because he had been shown the right, and had refused it.

It was at this time that revival meetings were organized in Portland, and Robert attended them with other members of the family. Several nights went by without response on the boy's part to the appeals of the evangelist; but on the sixth night, when the call to decide for Christ was made, he left his seat and went forward with others in public acknowledgment of his quest. He did not immediately find the satisfaction he sought, however. "If your father promised to do something for you, would you not believe him?" the evangelist asked, to which Robert replied that he certainly would. "Then will you not believe God when He promises to save you if you believe on the Lord Jesus Christ?"

Doubtless it was so clear to the evangelist that he could not understand Robert's inability to grasp elementary Gospel truth. But the boy went home without any conviction that he was saved. That night, however, as he lay in bed, his mind was stabbed with the thought: "I am still on my way to hell! I must do something, or I shall perish!" What had the preacher said? That God's promise was: "Believe on the Lord Jesus Christ, and thou shalt be saved." In an agony of fear the cry rose from his heart: "I will believe God! I cannot take the chance of going any further without Him!"

It is many years ago since that cry went up from the youthful sinner, but to this day R. G. recalls the joy which he experienced as he realized that God had answered his prayer, a joy which sent him posthaste to his mother's bed, there to break the news that he had made his peace with God.

"Mother! It's all settled now! You needn't pray

for me any more. I'm saved! And, Mother! Though I wouldn't submit to you or Dad, I must submit to God, and He says I must obey you, so with His help I will."

It was Elizabeth's testimony that on that night "the lion was turned into a lamb". Under the influence of the Spirit of God self-will gave place to consideration for others, headstrong obstinacy was tamed until he was willing to accept advice, and friends who were like millstones about his neck were discarded for Christian companions, with whom he shared the service of the Lord. Incidentally, shortly after Robert's conversion, his principal chum in his unregenerate days landed in jail, justifying his description of himself as "a brand plucked from the burning".

For the next sixteen years, Robert lived that sort of Christian life which, by the standards of today, would be judged normal, but only because the Church of Christ as a whole has departed so far from New Testament precept and practice. He went to church. He gave to the collection. He undertook small responsibilities. He believed that he was saved and on the way to heaven—but for all that was dynamic or effective in his Christian testimony other men and women might be lost.

To rebuke him for his lukewarmness there was the example of his younger sister, Marie (now Mrs. Tom Olson). "Bobby," she would say to him, "don't you *love* Jesus?" He shrunk from that deliberate emphasis, as did one of old when the Lord Himself made similar inquiry: "Simon, son of Jonas, lovest thou Me?" The test of Simon Peter's devotion was to be self-denying service; and by this same test Robert knew that his love for Christ was a poor, wilted thing compared with the fragrant flower which bloomed in his sister's heart. Did she not love the Lord well enough to go to the Indians of Arizona to tell them of His power to save? And was she not willing to go even further—to distant China—to deliver the same message?

"I knew that I ought to be witnessing for my Lord" —we are quoting Robert's own testimony—"for He had done so much for me. I tried to speak for Him, but I seemed unable to do it. The man working alongside me in the shop would take the name of my Lord in vain, and I would say nothing. I said to myself: 'If someone made fun of my mother or my sister I would not stand for it; yet I am allowing the name of my Lord and Saviour, who died for me on Calvary, to be taken in vain, and I make no protest.' Then one night I went to the altar again. I said: 'Lord, I need victory. I know the love that ought to be in my heart is not there. If You will give me the backbone that I need and fill me with Your Spirit so that I can witness for You, I'll do whatever You ask me from this day on.' And my Saviour took me at my word. I rose from my knees feeling that God had heard and answered. You may call that experience by any name you wish, but I say God heard and answered my prayer."

The occasion of this was another revival campaign, this time at Stockton. A call went out for reconsecration, and Robert answered by going forward that all might know how dissatisfied he was with the past, and how determined, by God's help, to do better in the future. The next morning he presented himself early at the home of his pastor.

"Brother, do you think that I should go out as a missionary?"

In his zeal to interpret his love for Christ in action, it seemed that he must answer the same call as Marie and his other sister, Sarah, and offer himself for service overseas. It might be that his age would disqualify him; but having promised the Lord to perform whatever was the divine will for his life, he was anxious to make good that promise, and was not prepared to interpose difficulties of his own creation.

"Let's pray about this, Bob," was his pastor's helpful suggestion.

So on their knees together the two men sought to discover God's purpose for this rededicated life. And who can doubt from all that followed that the necessary wisdom was granted? For when they rose to their feet again, Robert was challenged with words which were accepted as a revelation from Heaven, and which produced an immediate response from his willing heart.

"Bob, God needs business men as well as missionaries."

Shades of the Damascus road! "I was not disobedient unto the heavenly vision," was the Apostle Paul's glad testimony concerning the plan for his life which came through the lips of Ananias. And because of his ready response flood-tides of blessing were released upon a parched and weary world. So, in varying degrees and a multitude of ways, God has used the consent of men to His program for their lives as the channel through which to achieve His purposes of grace for multitudes. It was thus with Paul; and time would fail me to tell of Augustine, and of Columba, and Wyclif, and of Luther; of Moody also . . . and of Robert Gilmour LeTourneau.

"Bob, God needs business men as well as missionaries."

That was the call; and this the answer, eagerly and sincerely given from a heart which had no knowledge of the wonderful experience into which it would lead, but which was only anxious to find a way whereby it could repay its debt of love—

"Then I will do my best to be God's business man."

That is R. G.'s program and ambition still. You have heard others describe him as "God's Business Man"; but you have not heard him speak thus of himself. Still in line with the Apostle Paul he can say: "I count not myself to have apprehended . . . but I press toward the mark." The resolve of the young man of thirty-two, with his career as yet unmade, is the resolve of the successful executive who stands at the head of an enterprise valued in many millions: *I will do my best to be* God's business man."

And now that note of high endeavor has been struck we can proceed with our story, which from this point onward becomes not so much the record of the development of a successful business (though it is that), as a testimony to what God can do for and through a man who puts first things first.

What we have to relate is not an uncheckered progress, as though once a life is yielded to God it is automatically spared all that is disappointing and disagreeable. That is no part of the covenant of God with His people, and it is equally foreign to R. G. LeTourneau's Christian philosophy. He has never suggested that serving the Lord has been in his case an insurance against testing and trial; on the contrary, he has had these in plenty, and may have more ahead. What he does testify to others out of his experience is that "the angel of the Lord encampeth round about them that fear Him, and delivereth them", so that as one who has often been delivered he can join in the psalmist's chorus: "O taste and see that the Lord is good: blessed is the man who trusteth in Him."

CHAPTER V

A BIGGER SHOVEL

R. G. LETOURNEAU is in business as a land-levelling contractor by intention, and a manufacturer by force of circumstances. We must proceed to describe how, in response to an increasing demand for his machines, he decided to concentrate upon their production; how this new policy prospered; and how a small business, conducted in a field at the side of his home, grew and grew until it took its place among the large industrial concerns of the United States.

A field at the side of his home? Yes, that was the improvised way in which he began. It says much for California weather (almost as much, in fact, as Californians claim for it) that this open-air "shop" was possible for as long as a year; but the owner of the embryo business soon saw that if he was to take advantage of the opportunities which were being thrust upon him he must take steps to provide at least a roof over his head. So, in May, 1921, he built his first manufacturing plant at 122 Moss Avenue, Stockton, which still stands, and is affectionately known as the "old Moss Avenue shop". There R. G. and a loyal team of employees (for by now he had gathered round him a company of kindred spirits, some of whom are with him today occupying positions of importance in his vast concern) interpreted his ideas in revolutionary earth-moving equipment for some part of each year, and for the other part tested the machines which they made on the various jobs which were successfully negotiated.

It was a strenuous life, to be sure, but it brought high rewards. The story spread like wildfire of a man who used his own machinery to move dirt faster than was thought possible; and this reputation resulted in orders, which very soon exhausted the capacity of the Moss Avenue shop, so that it began to overflow its walls—and once again R. G. and his men were working in the open air.

Considering the diversions introduced by frequent contracting jobs, an almost incredible list of machines —each new one an improvement on its predecessor— came from that modest factory. On the human side, it was only possible because of the untiring energy of R. G. himself, enabling him not only to design the equipment but also to direct and assist in its manufacture, and then to superintend its operations when out on contract, plus the fact that he and his workers were a happy team, enthused by the example of their chief, and sharing his keenness to achieve new records. It was an education in democratic industrialism to see this band of brothers at their task, in which there were subordinates but no inferiors, a condition which expressed itself in the friendly familiarity of first names, even the boss being "Bob" to the rest. Visitors to the factories of R. G. LeTourneau Inc. are sometimes surprised to meet the same informality of relationship.

Maybe it could be defended by impressive psychological arguments; but the plain truth is that R. G. not only believes in a fraternal atmosphere in business, but creates it. You simply cannot stand on your dignity when he is around.

For nine years the Moss Avenue shop, with its open-air annex, served the purposes of the growing firm; but in 1930 it became imperative to find larger premises. By now the business was soundly established, and in 1929 it had been incorporated under the laws of California. It was accordingly decided to erect a new building, for which a site was obtained on Roosevelt Street and School Street, Stockton.

That building was of uncommon interest, because it embodied and justified one of R. G.'s engineering convictions, namely, that welding could be adapted to most constructional purposes. The structure which he raised, therefore, measuring 60 by 300 feet, was all-welded, undoubtedly the first of its kind. There was not a bolt, a screw or a nail used in its construction. Other buildings for which similar claims are made incorporate stone and wood, the term "all-welded" only referring to the steel-work which forms a proportion of the materials used. But the Roosevelt Street shop was built entirely of structural steel with corrugated iron welded to the structure.

How rapidly the business was expanding at this time is revealed by the fact that before the new plant was completed the original plans had to be revised and the size of the structure was doubled. Thus the habitual overflow into the open air was anticipated, and for a while the factory operations were contained within four walls. But only for a while, for when it became necessary to make an extension to the building this was erected over men who were working out in the California sunshine.

A glance at the company's ledgers for this period furnishes impressive information upon the rapid strides that were made. In 1930, the year in which the new plant was erected, sales totalled nearly $111,000, with a net profit of $34,474. In 1932 sales had practically doubled, and profits had risen to over $52,000. Next year brought an unprecedented increase both in sales and profits; but in 1934 the advance was phenomenal, sales falling little short of a million dollars, with profits exceeding $340,000.

Attribute this success to enterprise and ability if you will (and unquestionably credit is due to these), nevertheless Mr. LeTourneau has his own explanation. "From the minute I made God my business partner," he says, "things started to go." That is, he reckons the days of progress leading to prosperity from that memorable morning when, in the home of his pastor, he rose from his knees to declare: "I will do my best to be God's business man."

What, we may ask, was involved in that pledge? Primarily that he would seek to demonstrate in his life the possibility of taking Christian standards into the workaday world. That meant fairness toward employees, toward customers, toward competitors, toward all, in fact, with whom he had relations in the process of manufacturing, contracting, buying and selling. But this was not the limit of his acknowledged obligation. Two of his sisters had dedicated their lives to the work of the Gospel, and he had been willing to do the same. Instead, God had directed him into business, and it was his conviction that whatever gains accrued belonged not to him but to God, and were therefore to be used for God's work.

By way of illustrating this twofold responsibility and how it was discharged we draw upon experiences of the years of business expansion which we have just been describing. Early in 1931, R. G. had lost heavily upon an earth-moving contract, due to no fault of his own. When in the second half of that year he had a further contract to build the Orange County Dam, in Southern California, he found it necessary to seek financial help, and in consequence accepting a nominee of the bonding company to supervise operations in their interests.

Such a condition was only accepted, as may be imagined, under necessity, and R. G. found it irksome to have to consult a second opinion upon work with which he was so familiar. But a further irritant arose in the form of a State official, who declared that the contract had been begun too late in the year, with the rainy season impending, and that it must be abandoned until the following year, to prevent possible loss of life and property.

R. G. was certain that he could complete his work

before the rains came, and pointed out that to postpone
the task would add to his financial embarrassment,
with every possibility of ruining him. At last, the
State official agreed that if within one month he could
put 400,000 cubic yards of earth into the base of the
dam, that would be accepted as proof that he could
complete the job within the safety margin.

Four hundred thousand cubic yards in a month!
That was exactly twice the quantity that had been
estimated, and the proposition looked impossible. But
so much depended upon it that R. G. and his men determined to do their best. They would work day and
night, for seven days a week; and if they could attain
their target for the test month, then, by maintaining
the same effort they could complete the work before the
fine weather was ended.

At the end of the month the base was completed.
Everybody agreed that a record had been set up, and
there was general satisfaction. The only person who
was unhappy about things was R. G. He did not like
success purchased at the expense of Sunday labor. He
believed in the divine ordinance of one day's rest in
seven, and only the demands of an exceptional circumstance had made him waive his objections to a seven-
day week. He was not sure that he had been right in
giving way on this point; but he was quite sure that
the practice should continue no longer. Other contractors might have no scruples in this matter; but
if he was to be God's business man he must observe
God's laws.

One answer to "How does he do it?" is the airplane Mr. LeTourneau flies up to 5,000 miles a week for business and the Gospel. Here he is with his Lockheed "Lodestar." *(Plate XIII.)*

When visiting his plants, Mr. LeTourneau is usually to be found at his drawing-board in consultation with one or more of his engineers. He is the designer of all the equipment that bears his name.

So he told the overseer of the bonding company that Sunday work must stop. He was sure, he said, that his men could do as much work in six as they could in seven days, and that the contract would be completed on time. But that gentleman was not impressed. "Seven days a week," he declared, "or we take over the job."

This was a situation to refer to the Senior Partner, and after prayer R. G. was convinced that he must adhere to his principles whatever the consequences. So word was passed among the men that there would be no Sunday work, and when the day came round not one reported for duty—except the bonding company's representative and his assistant.

Of course, the situation was reported to the bonding company, and early on Monday morning the chief executive was on the telephone demanding an explanation. That R. G. had no difficulty in giving: as a Christian he regarded Sunday as God's day, and wished his men to enjoy its advantages. But the other man only stormed his protest, and threatened the worst if the seven-day week was not reintroduced. "Either that," he said as he hung up, "or we take over, and out you go."

It certainly looked as though the bonding company not only had the intention but also the power to carry out its threat. But, with another Sunday approaching, R. G. was resolved not to surrender. He laid his case before God, and resigned himself to the issue. Then, in the middle of the week, the chief executive, who in

his telephone conversation had expressed his determination to take over the matter personally, arrived
at the dam. It looked as though the crisis had come.
But to R. G.'s amazement the visitor put out his hand.
"Go ahead," he said, "and I will stand behind you."

Not to this day can R. G. tell what happened between
San Francisco and the Orange County Dam to account
for that unexpected change of attitude. But because
he believed in God and in the efficacy of prayer he is
sure that the Lord intervened, transforming an adversary into a friend.

The dam was finished on time, and the profits contributed substantially toward placing the company in
a sound financial position. A courageous stand for
Christian principles in business had been fully vin-
dicated.

Before we tell the second story, there is a background to supply. "Not this year, but next," R. G.
had said, "I will pay my dues to God. *This* year I
will make money, and *next* year I will give it." But
when next year came he was facing bankruptcy! That
was an experience he never forgot. From it he learned
that one of the key words in the vocabulary of faith
is the word *now*. In the postponement of our obligations there is always the element of danger. When
we say "Wait!" to God we always run risks.

So to our story. If we open the company ledgers
again we shall find that the record of progress is not
unbroken. In 1931, owing in part to circumstances
already mentioned, and again in part to the prevailing

economic depression, money was lost, and debts had accumulated to the value of hundreds of thousands of dollars. R. G.'s advisers were in favor of bowing to the inevitable, and filing his petition in bankruptcy. But he asked for time.

Sunday came round, the final day of the missionary convention at the church where R. G. attended. People were making their pledges for missions, and the urgent question before R. G. was what to do in the circumstances. Should he pledge the $5,000 which had been his practice? To do so would invite misunderstanding and criticism, for there were men in the meeting who were in his employ, and who had received no pay for five weeks. Even though his name as donor might be suppressed, everybody would know the source of such a sum. Yet not to pledge would be to go back upon the principle of his life, summed up in the words: "Seek ye first the kingdom of God and His righteousness, and all these things shall be added unto you."

When Nehemiah was in need of urgent wisdom he offered a swift and spontaneous prayer to God. That is what R. G. did in his dilemma, and incidentally that is what he has done throughout his life, not only in great emergencies, but in his hour-to-hour need of guidance and control. In the midst of an ultra-busy life he has cultivated the privilege of ready access into the presence of God, and at his drawing-board, in a directors' meeting, or on the public platform, he constantly uses the facility of God's ever-open door.

"Lord, what shall I do?" he asked, and almost immediately the thought came to him that he could make his pledge in the names of his children, and thus avoid the undesirable publicity which a large gift would bring. When he told his book-keeper that he was going to meet his full missionary obligation of $5,000, the answer he received was: "Then you might as well give up."

About this time he was having difficulty with a customer to whom he had sold a machine. The customer complained that it would not do the job, but R. G. was sure that it would, and introduced pneumatic tires as the solution of the problem. (The whole story of using pneumatics for earth-moving machinery is reserved for a later chapter.) The result was the complete satisfaction of the customer, who immediately ordered another machine. That set a problem for R. G., who had nothing to offer from stock, and no capital to pay for production. So he mentioned his difficulty, and suggested a small payment in advance. To his surprise, the customer sat down and wrote him a check for the full amount, enabling him to return home with sufficient to make substantial payment to his creditors and to meet his missionary pledge. "Such a thing," he says, "had never happened before, and has never happened since."

To people who express amazement at the amount of money which he gives to Christian work, Mr. LeTourneau often quotes the experience of another, who said: "I shovel in, and the Lord shovels out, only He uses a bigger shovel." That certainly is

R. G.'s testimony. Whatever the measure in which he has honored God he has been abundantly recompensed. In the five years from 1930 onward both sales and profits were multiplied ten times—and still his business grew. Even the new shop on Roosevelt Street became inadequate, and the question arose as to whether he ought not only to expand but to open up business in the industrial east. For several reasons his thoughts turned toward Peoria, in the State of Illinois, where, early in 1935, a site was purchased.

Long, long years before, when the LeTourneaus were still living in their native France, adventurous Frenchmen had reached this part of the country, and had decided that there they would make their home. On a promontory commanding a splendid view of the western bank of the Illinois River they built Fort Crevecoeur. Nothing but an inscribed stone now marks the site of this settlement. In the course of a few years, community life was transferred to the western bank, where it has remained since the close of the seventeenth century, under the flags successively of France, Britain and America. Today, the delightful prospect of open country which pleased the eyes of La Salle in 1680 is overbuilt with houses, shops, factories and distilleries, concerning which last a contemporary writer has claimed that the volume of the river "is as nothing to what Peoria turns out in liquor".

Although whiskey is one of the chief products of Peoria, however, it is by no means the only product, for innumerable articles of more commendable character pour from its factories. The fact that the Caterpillar Tractor Company was already established in the city weighed with R. G. in his decision to build in Peoria, for at that time his scrapers were being paired with Caterpillar equipment.

In the early months of 1935, therefore, we see R. G. and a band of Californian stalwarts surveying the riverside plot which had been acquired for the Peoria plant. It was not an encouraging sight. Every day for the first week after their arrival it poured with rain, so that they could not do much more than stand and gaze at the water-logged field where they must raise their factory, install their equipment, provide a railroad siding, and do everything else incidental to starting production.

But in such circumstances energetic leadership can achieve marvels, and that leadership was forthcoming. Applying himself to the task with all the ingenuity and verve of which he was capable, R. G. inspired the rest to almost superhuman performance. In less than a month the necessary siding was in, foundations had been laid for a small factory, machines and tools were being assembled—and, faithful to tradition, a start with production was being made in the open air. Thirteen scrapers were actually built during that first month, an achievement which set the tempo for the days ahead.

Before a year had passed it was necessary to double the accommodation. Twelve months after that it was doubled once again, so that the plant now measured 1,200 feet long. In 1941 a fresh extension was added, this time a steel and glass structure 160 feet wide, resulting in a total length of nearly a quarter-of-a-mile. But still business increased, and larger premises were called for, the need being met by further extensions in 1940, 1942 and 1943.

The year 1936 marked the most impressive development of the Peoria premises, and when his building was ready, R. G. invited the public to a service of dedication. This was a new idea to most, and some were ready to criticize; but the man responsible had no misgivings in his own mind about the appropriateness of his action, for this factory was to do something more than produce machines for shifting dirt; it was to furnish funds for the prosecution of Gospel witness in all parts of the earth. What more appropriate, then, than to commend the project to the blessing of Heaven?

But let R. G. speak for himself. On the occasion of this service of dedication he said:

"Some people may wonder what religion has to do with business? A number of years ago I asked myself the question: 'What is the use of having a religion that doesn't work?' The Spirit of the Lord spoke to me, and I realized that while I professed to love the Lord Jesus Christ, my actions did not prove it. I professed to have a Saviour who was able to help me, and at the same time I went worrying along in my own strength. I said to myself: 'If God is what I claim He is, why not go into partnership with Him?' I got down on my knees, and made a deal with God.

"I feel I could have kept my part of that deal much better than I have. But this business and its unparalleled growth show that God has done His part. A few years ago my creditors were trying to decide whether to give us a chance to pay up or to take their loss on the LeTourneau account. Now we are dedicating this second addition to our eastern factory, and doubling our production capacity in an effort to keep up with orders.

"You see we have a personal God, a personal Saviour. Isn't it marvellous that He is willing to condescend to make a personal deal with you and me, the creatures of His hand? If I did not seek to give God the glory and tell the world that this business really belongs to Him, seeking to honor Him in the dedication of this splendid new building, I would not be fulfillng my part of the deal.

"On the other hand, I would not seek to lower His grace to the level of a bargain. The Lord Jesus Christ, in shedding His precious blood to wash away our sins, has done that which we can never repay. But because I believe that God wants business men, as well as preachers, to be His servants, I believe that a factory can be dedicated to His service as well as a church, and that it can be the means of saving many souls.

"I believe that the world is looking for a religion that really works, and while I realize that success is not always to be measured in dollars and cents, any more than true joy and happiness can be measured that way, I am certain that if those who profess the name of Christ would really put their confidence in Him, they would find that God would not fail them."

Certainly God did not fail His servant who thus publicly declared his faith in Him. Turn back the pages of that ledger again! For the year 1935 sales totalled two million dollars, and profits well over half-a-million; in 1936 sales passed the four million figure, and profits rose to $1,364,393; next year and the next showed a continued upward trend, until, by 1940, the sales of this company had exceeded ten million dollars, with a profit approaching two millions. But that was not the peak, for a year later sales figures had been nearly doubled; and by 1944, R. G. LeTourneau Incorporated recorded total takings of over forty-two million dollars.

Nobody has been more surprised by this amazing success than the founder of the business himself. Speaking at the Peoria Chamber of Commerce soon after his arrival in that city he said that he looked forward to the time when he might employ sixty to seventy men. How could he foresee that the day was coming when he would have 3,000 on his pay-roll at Peoria alone, with almost twice that number when his other factories were included? At that time, of course, R. G.'s plans did not extend further than from Stockton, California, to Peoria, Illinois. How he came to erect three other factories in the Deep South is a story deserving to begin on a fresh page.

CHAPTER VI

IN THE DEEP SOUTH

ONE DAY in Omaha, Nebraska, two men sat on the same platform of a public meeting, awaiting their turn to deliver their addresses. They were complete strangers to one another, one being a Presbyterian minister who hailed from the Southern State of Georgia, and the other an industrialist whom we now know with some degree of intimacy, Robert Gilmour LeTourneau.

R. G. knew nothing about his companion, but he liked his message that day, and remarked upon it afterwards to a friend. Then he learned more. Dr. R. A. Forrest was not only a minister; he was also a pioneer in Christian education. Away down in Toccoa Falls, among the mountains of northern Georgia, he had started a school where boys and girls could receive a sound education combined with instruction in the Bible, as a preparation for Christian service. At that time—the year was 1911—there was no similar institution south of the Mason-Dixon Line.

The principles of that school, as explained to him, greatly appealed to R. G.'s practical mind, and he was further interested when he learned that Dr. Forrest had passed through Omaha on his way to Seattle, where he was to sail for the Far East, in order to gain first-hand experience of missionary activities there. The sudden thought that here was a man who could be trusted to act on his behalf by conveying gifts direct to missionaries on the field prompted R. G. to despatch a check by air mail to Dr. Forrest, which he received on reaching Seattle. It was for $1,000, and Dr. Forrest was given absolute liberty of action in disposing of it.

Months passed, and then one day a small package arrived on Mr. LeTourneau's desk. It consisted of a wad of receipts, every one of them for small amounts of ten or twenty dollars, with signatures which represented mission stations spread over a very wide area. Wherever Dr. Forrest had gone he had left a token of Christian remembrance and generosity in R. G. LeTourneau's name, a veritable trail of sunshine. And in discharge of his stewardship he had obtained a signed acknowledgment for each gift, so that the donor might know exactly how his thousand dollars had been expended.

"Come and see me when you're this way," wrote Mr. Le Tourneau, by way of acknowledging the receipts, and in due course Dr. Forrest called at Peoria, and the two men discovered how much they had in common. By this means acquaintance developed into mutual admiration, and admiration into friendship. Some time later the Toccoa Falls Institute received a gift of $10,000 drawn on R. G.'s account, and the gift was followed, after a brief interval, by a visit to the school.

The visit put ideas into R. G.'s head. He found the Institute situate in the most delightful country, enjoying the advantages of a kindly climate, and catering to many mountain children who otherwise could not have experienced the blessing of a Christian education. He also learned that the Institute's curriculum gave a considerable place to vocational training, which was entirely in accord with his own ideas on how to teach the young. "What a fine thing it would be," he thought, "if some of these mountain lads could gain practical engineering experience while continuing their studies under the supervision of Dr. Forrest."

The fact was that at this time the capacity of the Peoria plant was being overtaxed, and it seemed nothing less than good business to contemplate opening a new factory. Why not at Toccoa? True, the industrialization of the Southern States was only slowly advancing, but many business men were persuaded of the desirability and wisdom of introducing manufacturing plants there, and with R. G. there was the additional reason that he would be assisting Dr. Forrest's worthy plan for the promotion of better conditions among the mountain folk.

So, in November, 1938, Peoria sent out a pioneering party to commence the construction of a new plant on a site not far distant from the small town of Toccoa, Georgia. In little over six months it was possible to hold a service of dedication, attended by a crowd so large that it was the talk of the district for long afterward. There R. G. LeTourneau reaffirmed his faith in God, and pleaded with men and women to give their hearts to Jesus Christ. Neither were the physical needs of the crowd forgotten that day, for at a barbecue following the dedication, twenty hogs and thirty sheep were roasted and eaten, plus fourteen hundred pounds of beef, washed down by what seemed an unlimited supply of soft drinks; which is a way they have in "Dixie", and who shall say that it is not an excellent way?

But what followed was best, though it surely stamped the opening of this factory as the most remarkable event of its kind ever known. For night after night revival meetings were held for the benefit of Toccoa and district, at which hundreds accepted the Lord Jesus Christ as Saviour. At the close of each service, R. G. was to be seen upon his knees, seeking to lead some other soul into the blessing which he possessed.

An early development at Toccoa was the provision of housing for employees, by which means a new community sprang up around the plant, complete with its own stores, medical and recreational facilities, dairy farm, and later its own hotel. Moreover, to the natural beauties of the area Mr. LeTourneau made an addition in the form of a lake, which he named after his only daughter, Louise. We cannot have it thought that this lake was constructed just for the fun of the thing, for R. G. does not believe in the ornamental apart from the useful; so we hasten to explain that Lake Louise came into existence through the construction of a dam over a local mountain stream, upon which LeTourneau equipment could be tested under really stiff conditions. That dam has now become a fine highway, and the waters which it imprisons have filled a valley, and have thus been transformed into a stretch of inland water which challenges the suggestion that any other hand than Nature's own was the designer.

Lake Louise covers 185 acres, and has a shore-line of twenty-five miles. On this shore, at a spot admirably chosen, the Lake Louise Hotel has been built to the original design of Mr. LeTourneau. The hotel is in the shape of a star, with a large circular auditorium in the center, from which proceed seven radials —one functioning as a dining-hall, and the rest providing bedrooms and other necessary accommodation.

The central auditorium declares the true purpose of this lakeside hotel, for while a passing traveler may obtain "bed, bath and breakfast", or prolong his stay for as long as he wishes to enjoy the charms of northern Georgia, the real objective is Christian and spiritual. Lake Louise Hotel is a conference center, and as such is in increasing use by Evangelical groups who are full of admiration for its catering, its comfort, its auditorium accommodation (as many as 1,700 can be seated) and the natural beauty with which it is surrounded.

An annual event, sponsored by Mr. LeTourneau himself, is a summer Bible Conference, designed to give instruction and experience in various forms of Gospel testimony. Although at its beginning, this conference promises to meet a need in the South, by fostering a spirit of interdenominational co-operation and fellowship. Lake Louise is also increasingly used as a conference center by various Evangelical Societies and groups.

Thus R. G. LeTourneau came to Georgia, and thus he brought advantage after advantage to a small and relatively poor community, among whom for a time he and Mrs. LeTourneau made their home. On a well-chosen site overlooking Lake Louise they built their house, though it was not for long to be personally occupied and enjoyed. There were new fields to conquer!

Before we leave Tournapull, however, by which name this self-contained township, gathered around the LeTourneau factory, has come to be known, we have a sad duty to discharge by visiting the little cemetery on the hill, where, in Georgia's red soil, rests the body of Donald Philip, eldest son of Robert and Evelyn LeTourneau, killed in a 'plane accident on August 19, 1940, only three months after his marriage. Don had been a student at the Toccoa Falls Institute, and then had joined his father in the business, showing great promise as an engineer, and what was even more gladdening for his parents, proving himself a true follower of Jesus Christ. The modest stone erected over his resting-place bears the words "The Lord is my Shepherd, and I am His sheep"— this young man's last public testimony to his faith.

The somewhat bold step which R. G. LeTourneau took when he decided to build a factory in "Dixie" apparently brought no disillusionments or regrets, for four years later we find him planning yet another in the South. This time he looked in the direction of Mississippi. His ideal site, already exemplified in Peoria, was a place enjoying the threefold advantages of river, road and rail: and by this test he was attracted to the historic city of Vicksburg.

The epic of Vicksburg is commemorated in a date. By America as a whole, July 4 is preserved as Independence Day, marking the final severance from Britain and declaring the right and intention of the Colonists to govern themselves. But in Vicksburg, July 4 is an anniversary of very different sort, for on that day, in the year 1863, the Confederate forces which had held the city against the repeated assaults of the Union army finally surrendered to General Grant, after a siege lasting forty-seven days and nights. This was a decisive victory for Grant, for it opened up the Mississippi Valley to his control. Port Hudson fell five days later, and thus the chief objective of the Western Campaign was won, and the backbone of the Confederacy was broken. It may be readily understood that the citizens of Vicksburg found it difficult to join the rest of the United States in keeping July 4 as a day of flag-waving and holiday; indeed, when the present writer was in Vicksburg in July, 1947, Independence Day was being celebrated for the third occasion only—and then under the title of "The Carnival of the Confederacy".

About eleven miles south of the battle-lines of Vicksburg, still preserved as a National Military Park,

Mr. LeTourneau purchased the old Glass Plantation, in whose cotton fields hundreds of negro slaves had once toiled, and around which many of their liberated descendants still lived. The year was 1942, and war had again come to America, not this time setting State against State and brother against brother, but uniting all Americans in a common struggle against tyrannies which threatened the overthrow of democracy. LeTourneau, of course, was in it! At Peoria and Toccoa his factories were helping to supply the sinews of war. Another factory would considerably step-up this vital production.

But war creates shortages, and shortages are accompanied by restrictions, so that when R. G. proposed to erect his Vicksburg premises he was met by various hindrances, chief of which was that he might only use materials already in hand. This, however, was the sort of challenge to ingenuity which he welcomed. There was no lack of timber on the site, so trees were cut and sawn on the spot to provide walls for the factory. These walls were so constructed that they were hinged from the top, and could be raised upwards and outwards for the admission of air—a measure made necessary because of the intense humidity of the district. As for the roof, that had to be made from available metal, consisting mainly of short lengths, which were welded together after R. G.'s own design. The result has proved so satisfactory that what was produced under necessity has been reproduced elsewhere.

Building the Vicksburg plant also gave opportunity

for LeTourneau scrapers, bulldozers and other equipment to prove their mettle. The ground level of the actual site had to be raised from six to eight feet—a prodigious task for contractors of a past decade, but all in the day's work for these machines with their insatiable appetite for dirt. A neighboring hill was sacrificed and transferred to where it could serve a utilitarian purpose; and atop the transported soil the new factory rose.

That operation had its disadvantages, for the area was ankle-deep in mud during the winter, and hidden by clouds of dust in summer—and nothing could be done about it. There was a war on! But these discomforts have now been overcome by the provision of good roads. A fine administrative building has been added, complete with an effective air-conditioning system, which is much appreciated by the staff when the mercury rises in the thermometer. And away up the hill which overlooks the factory dozens of modern dwellings have been erected for the convenience of the workers, the topmost being for the accommodation of the LeTourneau family.

It is pleasant to think of them enjoying the facilities of that hill-top home, with its commanding view of the winding Mississippi, its semi-tropical vegetation and insect life, its . . . But what's the use? The urge to build again has already thrust them forth, and the Vicksburg home has passed into the occupancy of the plant manager, while the LeTourneaus accommodate themselves in the erstwhile ward of a U. S. Army hospital, way down in Longview, Texas.

Why Texas? That is a story all its own, and one which we will reserve for another chapter, satisfying ourselves now by a description of the location of this fourth and latest factory.

Longview is a flourishing community situate in Gregg County, East Texas, the greatest oil-producing county in the United States. The East Texas oil-field was discovered in 1931, and today there are more than 25,000 active wells. Many stories are told in the district of men becoming wealthy overnight by the discovery of oil on their property; and there is one story about a church site upon which oil was located, resulting in an emergency meeting of the membership, at which it was unanimously resolved that no new members should be accepted. But that is probably apocryphal.

What is certain is that R. G. expected no overnight prosperity as a result of his arrival in Longview. Let other men find and sell oil; he would make the machines to consume it, without any dreams about sudden fortunes. But his coming certainly contributed to the prosperity of the local community, and resulted in its early enlargement. Bit by bit, Longview is moving out of town in the direction of the LeTourneau plant, which, though only laid down in 1946, has a high production figure. Youngest of the quartette of factories (the original plant at Stockton, California, is no longer used for manufacturing purposes), Longview nevertheless promises to be a most valuable company asset.

CHAPTER VII

MOVING THE EARTH

WE HAVE traced the development of a business from a back-yard shop to four large, modern factories, employing thousands of men, and the advancement of our "one-tool mechanic" from his humble beginnings to the presidency of a vast commercial organization representing millions of dollars. Now the question properly arises, as it has doubtless already arisen in the minds of some readers: What kind of machines are made in these factories? The term "earth-moving machinery" has been employed freely, and strange words like "bulldozer" and "scraper" have recurred; but is it possible to give the non-technical person a clearer idea of their significance?

One thing is certain, that it is not necessary to be technically-minded to appreciate the importance of earth-moving, for since "Adam delved and Eve span" this has been the constant occupation and problem of mankind. Whether making a garden, or building a house, or constructing a road, earth had to be dug and carted. As building schemes became more ambitious, and methods of communication developed, so the excavation and transporting of soil became more serious tasks.

There were modest little schemes like the pyramids, for example. In the absence of mechanized aid, the Pharaohs had their own solution in massed slave labor. Presumably it did not matter how long you employed man, or how many men you employed, when there were no wages to pay. But they had at least to be fed, and the Egyptian commissariat must have had many headaches over a contract which lasted thirty years before even the base of one pyramid was excavated.

That was the trouble in those days: earth-moving took an interminable time when the only available helps were men's hands, picks and shovels, buckets and baskets, pulleys and hoists, with unwilling animals and slow-moving vehicles to carry the dirt away. It has been estimated that it took 100,000 men working ten years to make a causeway 3,000 feet long for the conveyance of stone to be used on the construction of the Great Pyramid at Giza. Obviously, anybody who could have introduced a speedier method would have had a good reception.

But speedier methods were a long time coming. The invention of gunpowder, in the fifteenth century, made a contribution to the problem; but processes remained primitive until, by harnessing steam, men compelled a new power to work for them, and thus obtained a measure of relief from hard, manual labor. The steam scoop shovel, introduced in 1850, was the most revolutionary step forward for 400 years.

In 1859, when the Suez Canal was begun, men were still preferred to machines, though before that pro-

ject was completed, ten years later, mechanical help
was co-opted to hurry the task forward to completion.
Even so, the work of earth-moving was still arduous
and protracted, remaining so as late as the end of the
nineteenth century, when the final development of the
Panama Canal was pushed ahead by the United States
Government.   It is interesting to recall that ten years
were required before the canal was open to traffic, and
that 39,000 men were employed.   Though the quantity
of earth shifted in this undertaking was tremendous,
being estimated at over 220 million cubic yards at the
opening of the canal in 1914, the same operation could
be carried through today at infinitely less expenditure
of time, labor, health and money.

It was about six years after the opening of the
Panama Canal that, his garage days ended, Bob Le-
Tourneau tried his hand at levelling farmland.   By
then things had really progressed in the earth-moving
business.   Tractors had begun to displace mules, and
machines were introduced which could pick up 3 cubic
yards of dirt, and race away with them at the reckless
speed of $2\frac{1}{2}$ miles an hour, which, for 20 tons of steel,
was a creditable performance.   Imagine what a snail's
pace this must have seemed, however, to a man who
had been setting up records in automobile racing!

Was it surprising that, as he sat precariously perched
on this lumbering machine, R. G. should figure out
improvements, or that, as it groaned and clanked along,
he should produce ideas for a better performance at
higher speeds?   The first scraper which owned him as

its designer was a full-drag type, similar to the prevailing pattern. That was built in the spring of 1922, and by the summer he had second thoughts which expressed themselves in another machine, "The Gondola", welded throughout (of course!), and therefore lighter in weight than other dirt-shifting tools. Its superiority was further demonstrated by the fact that it had electric motors for loading and unloading, and that it could scoop up and carry 6 cubic yards.

When machine No. 3 came along it was the most ambitious departure from the small-capacity earthmover of that day. It was 12 feet wide, and had two four-foot buckets, the rear bucket telescoping inside the front. It was completed early in 1923, and was immediately nicknamed "The Mountain-Mover"—a stiff claim for a rig which picked up 15 or 16 yards of soil for a load. But since most people were still satisfied with one-fifth or even one-sixth of that quantity, it represented a big advance on contemporary ideas. "The Mountain-Mover" traveled on spoked iron wheels, and was pulled by a tractor. Clearly, it was built to last, for in 1944 it was still at work.

A common principle characterized these scrapers and their aristocratic successors: they were designed not only to scoop up earth at one point, and to dump it at another, but also to spread the unloaded earth to the precise depth required in smooth, even layers from 1 inch up to 16, 18, 20, or even (on some models) 22 inches. That primary purpose has been facilitated by all kinds of improvements. It has been possible to increase the size and capacity of the bowl, for example, into which the earth is scooped. Hard-surfaced cutting edges have been introduced, so that when the bowl is lowered into contact with the ground, its blade-like edge penetrates the hardest substances, like a knife going through butter. Then, methods of raising and lowering the bowl have been vastly improved, while by adding "aprons" and "gates" the gathered earth is securely contained within the bowl while being transported, and then mechanically dumped within a minimum of time.

The earliest scrapers had steel wheels. Then came tracks, similar to those used on tractors; but the weight proved a disadvantage, and they were discarded in favor of bigger and broader steel wheels. In 1932, a contractor using LeTourneau equipment in Imperial Valley, California (we are back at the incident mentioned in Chapter V), found the going so hard in the sand that he was for scrapping the machines and turning over to something else. R. G. persuaded him, however, to fit the rubber tires on which the machines had been brought over the road from the factory at Stockton. The contractor was slow to co-operate, but at length he fitted the tires, and the difficulty was overcome; in fact, from that time forward rubber tires became standard with LeTourneau earth-moving rigs. By teamwork between the LeTourneau Company and the Firestone Tire and Rubber Company giant tires have been produced to carry the heaviest machines over the worst ground. Bigger and bigger sizes, with less and less air pressure, have overcome many problems; and today the products of Peoria and the other factories use tires as big as 9 ft. 4 in. in height, with air pressure as low as 20 pounds.

As we have already mentioned, the prototypes of earth-moving machinery were pulled by mule, and if we go far enough back, we find them hand-guided, with animals hauling the scraper, and a man behind steering it by means of a handle, on the same principle as a plough. That method had its disadvantages for the human operator if the scraper struck a rock. Then the handle was liable to be jolted upward, flinging the wretched operator through the air in front of his hauling team. He is much better off today comfortably seated before push-button controls, by means of which he can make the enormous machine beneath him perform to his will.

For this is the amazing stage in the development of earth-moving machinery which has now been reached. In place of animal-haulage, and even superseding the tractor, R. G. has designed and introduced the *Tournapull*, a tough, high-powered, high-speed unit which can either pull or push giant appliances up hill or down dale, or wherever they are required to go. Linked with the LeTourneau *Carryall* scraper, the *Tournapull* will tackle earth-moving jobs with incredible performance, and enable one man to do what was impossible for an entire gang a few years ago. In fact, this combination of machines has been described as "the fourth major evolution in more than 5,000 years of earth-moving".

What we said about push-buttons is nothing less than the sober truth. Thanks to the genius of R. G. LeTourneau, the operator sits before a panel upon which is a row of electric buttons. The first two on his left give him two steering speeds. He moves a switch to the left or right to make a corresponding turn. Three buttons on his right control the three motors on the scraper, which operate the front apron, the tailgate and the bowl respectively. Other buttons represent the starter, the horn and manifold heat. Also on the panel are warning lights which register irregularities of oil pressure, and tell when the fuel supply is getting low.

During the 1920-30 period, earth-moving was accomplished by steam and gasoline units, and was necessarily slow. Using a 1,000 feet haul as basic, the average delivery was 8 cubic yards per man-hour, at a cost of about 50 cents per cubic yard. During the period 1930-33, the first true gasoline tractor was employed as a haul unit, and this increased production to a figure of 12 cubic yards per man-hour, at a cost of about 45 cents per cubic yard.

In 1933, when rubber tires were introduced, scraper performance was stepped up and production costs lowered. Hauling the same distance (1,000 feet) during 1933-39 meant a delivery of 60 cubic yards per man-hour, at a cost of about 14 cents per cubic yard.

When, in 1939, the *Tournapull* was invented a considerable saving both of time and money was effected. Production with this piece of equipment on a 1,000 feet haul is 130 cubic yards per man-hour, at a cost of 8 cents per cubic yard delivered.

These figures are eloquent, but they do not give the end of the story. One of R. G.'s favorite anecdotes concerns the Great Barnum, who, when asked what he would do if one of his circus wagons got into a ditch, replied: "Put on more horses." "Yes, Mr. Barnum," returned his inquirer, "but what if that failed to get the wagon out." "Put on more horses," the showman answered again. "But supposing even they failed to do the job, what then, Mr. Barnum?" And sticking to his guns, the answer was given back: "Put on more horses."

Acting upon this same principle, R. G. goes on adding "horses" to his machines to meet the need for equipment which will carry more dirt at even greater speeds. The baby of the *Tournapull* family is rated at a mere 85 horse-power. Next comes a sturdy youth possessing 150 horse-power. An even more robust member can boast 225 horse-power, though he has to take second place to a giant of 300 horse-power, known as the "A" model. It is rumored that, for all his strength, this monster is known to tremble at the sight of R. G. working at his drawing-board.

At the moment, however, the "A" *Tournapull,* paired with the "E50" *Carryall,* is the last word in earth-moving apparatus. It can travel at 18 miles an hour, with a top capacity of 40 cubic yards of earth, and delivers at a rate of 285 cubic yards per man-hour, at a cost of 7 cents per cubic yard.

That is progress! The facts presented another way may be almost more impressive. In 1920, one man operating through a ten-hour day could shift 50 yards of dirt 300 feet, using mules and a "Fresno" scraper, which was the type of earth-moving machine then in use. Now, an "A" *Tournapull* working with an "E50" *Carryall,* with one man operating, assisted by another man acting as driver to a spare *Tournapull* for serving three scrapers alternately, which we may express as one-man-and-a-third, can shift in one hour, over a 5,000-feet haul, 164 yards of sand, 145 yards of earth, or 127 yards of heavy clay.

Or again: a "station yard", in the parlance of earth-moving engineers, is one yard of earth moved 100 feet. The 1920 man working with his mule could convey 15 station yards per hour. The 1948 man with an "A" *Tournapull* moves (and not only moves, but also lifts and spreads) better than 12,000 station yards per hour.

A record for earth-moving with LeTourneau equipment was established in the construction of the Great Falls (Montana) Army Airbase. "The project," reads the official report, "was started June 8, 1942, with the stripping of vegetation in preparation for the actual dirt-moving. Three days later, heavy equipment was moved in for dirt operations. A month later, work had progressed sufficiently so that base gravel could be applied on the first runway, and a short time later asphaltic concrete pavement was being laid. Grading of the airport area was completed December 11, 1942, with more than 5,000,000 cubic yards of earth moved in a period of 188 days. On an average, 50,000 cubic yards of dirt were moved each day when all equipment was in operation. This task was accomplished despite unfavorable weather—snow, fog and sub-zero temperatures. In one twenty-four-hour period, 104,905 cubic yards of earth were moved on this project."

Although the *Tournapull* and *Carryall* are the most important products of LeTourneau plants, contractors throughout the world are grateful for a range of other devices which have proved their effectiveness and reliability under the most exacting conditions.

There is, of course, the bulldozer, the simplest of mechanical earth-moving machines, consisting of a heavy steel blade mounted horizontally upon a four-wheeled, rubber-tire tractor. The blade can be raised or lowered, and when it thrusts forward, digging into the ground, nothing can resist it. By sheer brute force it pushes all before it. For levelling ground, removing debris and even felling trees it is an invaluable piece of equipment. Bulldozers which are built in the LeTourneau factories have the inevitable name of *Tournadozers*.

For inflicting further punishment upon this poor old earth there are rooters and sheep's foot rollers, the former, as the name suggests, having steel teeth which tear up hard surfaces in advance of the scrapers, and the latter doing the work of a regiment of giants marching backwards and forwards over soft earth until it is stamped hard.

Then there are *Tournatrailers* for the transport of earth and rocks, or whatever is required to be shifted from one joint to another—massive vehicles, with a capacity of 17 cubic yards. *Tournatrailers* have wide tops for easy loading, and sliding bottoms or ends for the discharge of their contents. They are fitted with large rubber tires, which engage any surface; indeed, most men who drive them believe that they "would go up the side of a house." The *Tournatruck* is a flat conveyance for taking heavy loads, such as machinery. It is specially designed for off-the-road use and for negotiating the roughest country. Another member of this family of giants is the *Tournawagon*, which comes from the LeTourneau factories in three sizes, capable of containing 16, 33 and 40 tons respectively.

Tournacranes to which we may have other opportunity to refer, are among the brain-children of R. G., and are to be included in the output of the LeTourneau shops; *Tournalayers*, too, whose name does not so readily convey their purpose, for what they "lay" are houses, which amazing disclosure must be left for elaboration on a later page. And, though small by comparison with the mighty contrivances of wheels and gears which come from the same source, honorable mention must be given to *Tournaweld* (welding-rods made to satisfy the exacting standards of the arch-welder of all time) and *Tournarope* (wire, of course, and strong enough to stand up to the heavy work required of earth-moving machinery).

And lest this chapter should look too much like a catalogue we leave it at that, risking the omission of some things which should have been included, and hoping that enough has been written to enlighten those who are interested in such matters. At least we should now know something about the products of the Tourna-plants, as doubtless we have gained in appreciation of the inventive genius who is behind them.

Let us turn our attention to another theme of the interest and importance of which there can be no doubt: not machines, but marriage. For it is un-questionably time to introduce to our circle the lady who, for over thirty years, has been the helpmeet of Robert Gilmour LeTourneau.

Meet Mrs. LeTourneau!

CHAPTER VIII

AND NOW FOR ROMANCE

"BOB, WHAT are you doing carting that girl around with you every evening?"

"Doing, Dad? Why, nothing. I am working on cars all day, and the only chance I get to test them is at the end of the day. It's nice to have somebody with me."

"Bob, you're in love."

Caleb LeTourneau looked his son right in the eye as he said it, but Bob did not flinch. In love? The suggestion was ridiculous. Evelyn Peterson, his companion on these evening drives, was several years his junior. He had met her as a child of twelve at some revival meetings in Stockton, and a friendship had sprung up between them. But in love? Not that ... not yet.

Evelyn's father was a conscientious employee of a large Stockton firm, where some labor disputes incited a strike. Mr. Peterson, unable to reconcile his principles with participation in the strike, decided to remain at work. This annoyed the strikers, who laid wait for him in the street, and he would have sustained injury if he had not taken refuge in a friendly house. From there he sent a message to Bob LeTourneau, asking him to bring a car to fetch him. Thus Bob became the bodyguard of Evelyn's father, and in order

Portrait of R. G. LeTourneau (*Collier's Magazine*). Every week-end throughout the year, Mr. LeTourneau addresses thousands of people in audiences gathered to hear his Christian testimony.

These members of the LeTourneau staff have left their desks and machines for thirty minutes, in order to assemble in the canteen for a Gospel meeting. Every person on the pay-roll has the opportunity to attend such a meeting once a week—during company time.

to discharge his office more efficiently, accepted an invitation to take up residence in the Peterson house.

At this time, the little girl was about thirteen, and Bob LeTourneau a big strapping fellow. "Uncle Bob," she called him, and took the keenest interest in his welfare. In fact, when a love affair went wrong with him, Evelyn was among the first to express her sympathy, which Bob gladly accepted, and was surprised to discover how quickly he got over his disappointment under the solicitous attentions of his young friend.

Of course, Caleb was right. The difference in ages between Evelyn and Bob was not sufficient to prevent friendship deepening into love, and before long an embarrassed automobile mechanic presented himself before Mr. Peterson to acknowledge just how he felt toward his daughter.

So far, so good. But apparently Bob had not been precise enough in his approach to Evelyn's father, who, while prepared to view with approval from a distance the prospect of her marriage, had not brought himself to realize that Bob liked to get things done quickly, and was therefore thinking in terms of an early wedding. When the fact was pressed upon him by a return visit, he declared that Evelyn was too young, and that they must wait.

Bob frankly thought that he had waited long enough, but by an unusually successful effort of patience he managed to defer to Mr. Peterson's wishes for several months, after which he renewed his request, still to be met, however, by refusal. This was too much for him, and he said quite plainly that he thought the objection was unreasonable.

Evelyn thought so, too. There was reason to believe, in fact, that Mrs. Peterson thought so, and that she only supported her husband from a sense of wifely duty. In any case, the more the two young people talked about things, the more determined they were to get married, with Mr. Peterson's permission if possible, but if necessary without it. And since they lacked his permission, and were not likely to obtain it, they resolved upon a bold course. They would elope.

Doubtless we ought to draw a veil over this episode, or, if mentioning it, do so with a sense of restraint and with manifested disapproval. Admittedly, it was very naughty. . . . But look at them, making for the Mexican border in Bob's car, with the irate father in pursuit! Merced—Madera—Fresno—Bakersfield— the towns fly by! There can be no doubt how the chase will end, for you can teach Bob nothing about driving a car. Two hundred miles! Three hundred miles! Four hundred miles! Now Mexico is within easy reach, and the pursuit is off. Over the border and the day will be won! Tia Juana is ahead, and Tia Juana will do. . . .

Crave pardon! We are about to record that, on August 29, 1917, Robert Gilmour LeTourneau, mechanic, of Stockton, California, and Evelyn Peterson, spinster, of the same city, were joined in matrimony at Tia Juana, Lower California, Mexico. Back home in Stockton father-in-law Peterson nursed his bad feel-

ings for some six years, and then, at his own suggestion, "buried the hatchet". In the LeTourneau
household, the gentle Elizabeth calmed her husband's
agitation, and closed the matter finally for herself and
for him when she said: "It's done, and it cannot be
undone; and I am not going to be unhappy about it."

As the passing years quickly proved, there was
nothing to be unhappy about in the marriage of Bob
and Evelyn, for if ever God matched a woman to a
man, He did it for them. In the home, in business and
in Christian activity she is a perfect helpmeet, temp-
erament, ability and harmony of interest all contribu-
ting to an ideal partnership. Time has brought its
trials and its sorrows—their firstborn stayed with them
but four months, long enough to make a place in their
affections that none other could fill, and then slipped
away—but through them all two things have remained
steadfast: their faith in God and their love for one
another.

Their first home was the old Moss Avenue shop,
Stockton, where Evelyn not only kept house but also
acted as bookkeeper and ran errands, while Bob built
his first scraper in the driveway. He never had a
more willing helper. He only had to shout through
the kitchen window that he needed some more steel,
and Evelyn would get out the car, bundle the two
babies in beside her, and go out in search of the
necessary metal. She never returned without it. As
Bob got on with his job he would hear the old car
chugging homeward, the precious sheets and bars

clanging away in the special racks which he had built
on top and side.

How she managed to raise a family, assist in her
husband's business, and engage in various forms of
Christian work, nobody could tell.   That was Evelyn's
own secret, and it is one that is with her still.   As the
business grew she adapted herself to changing conditions, and constantly revealed new talents in response
to the challenge of circumstances.

When the first big advance was made in 1935,
Evelyn accompanied her husband to Peoria, not only
to look after him but to mother the party of young
men who were transferred from Stockton for the
purpose.   To them she was "Mom" and it was no
trouble to her to house twenty of them in her new
Peoria home, or to cook for double that number as
her contribution to the task in hand.   Later she started
the factory cafeteria, and for a time acted as chief
cook in a kitchen where food was prepared for about
three hundred people.

The opening of the Georgia plant brought new opportunities for service to youth, for there a machinists'
school was set up, having as many as seventy-five
young men in residence.   To them, Mrs. LeTourneau
was friend, confidante and adviser.   Though time has
scattered them, they still have a way of turning to her
in seasons of trouble or of joy; in fact, whenever
an experience comes along which they feel they must
share, it is to "Mom" they go, knowing that they will

find a sympathetic ear and a helping hand and a wise counsellor.

When the time came to move on to Vicksburg, Mississippi, Mrs. LeTourneau went with the pioneering party, and for a while had to live in nothing better than a shack. This was in sharp contrast to her attractive steel and glass house at Toccoa; but the position was cheerfully accepted until something could be done to provide better accommodation. Even then, it was largely a case of self-help, for the war was on, and labor was scarce. "I almost built it by myself," she says of the ranch-type dwelling, which tops a hill overlooking plant, air-strip and river.

At Vicksburg, Mrs. LeTourneau was able to bring a wider circle of young men under her influence. Around the city, within a one-hundred-mile radius, were many military camps, catering to thousands of American boys. At week-ends or whenever leaves permitted, they made for Vicksburg, in search of companionship and entertainment. Recognizing the dangers which beset them, Mrs. Letourneau saw also the need for a center where they could find true Christian hospitality, and began to look around for suitable premises.

A former funeral home, in the heart of historic Vicksburg, suggested itself as ideal for the purpose. The fact that this building possessed a chapel added to its suitability, for the intention was to provide for the spiritual as well as the physical needs of the visitors. Renamed "Fellowship Inn", these premises were adapted and opened for the benefit of servicemen, where they could obtain week-end accommodation or occasional meals at no cost. Those who used these facilities were expected to attend Sunday morning service, where many of them heard the Gospel if they had never heard it before. Hundreds of lads passed through the hospitable doors of "Fellowship Inn", and received there an experience of Christian living which could not fail to leave its impression.

When the march of events took the LeTourneaus from Vicksburg to Longview, this meant an even fuller opportunity for Mrs. LeTourneau, for there, in the Technical Institute of Texas (of which more hereafter) she found hundreds of ex-G.I.s, men who had given their service to their country, and were now seeking to equip themselves for civilian life. Making her home in their midst, she began among them that dual ministry of social and spiritual provision at which she has become expert. Once again she was "Mom", with hundreds of young lives to work upon for Christ. It is too early yet to assess the value of her presence there, for the work is in its infancy; but the possibilities are tremendous.

Through the years, Mrs. LeTourneau has shown an increasing interest in Youth Camps, and we may profitably retrace our steps to learn how she contracted this enthusiasm. Upon her own testimony, it really all began with a conviction that she ought to do something to win others for the Lord. She had been converted at the early age of twelve, but had shunned the responsibility of personal witness, leaving it, as she said, to preachers to talk to folk about salvation.

Seeking a method by which she might discharge this conscious obligation, she decided to invite her husband's Sunday School class to accompany her and her four children to the Mt. Hermon Camp, in the Santa Cruz Mountains of California. Thus she found herself in charge of a party of boys—"a tough gang" —of whom only one was a Christian. They had a great week together, filling the days with healthy fun, and attending the meetings which were held morning and evening. But if the boys were completely happy, their hostess was not. "Speak to them about the Lord," a voice within charged her; but the week sped by, and she failed to obey.

It was not until the night before they were due to return home that she found courage to speak. On the way up to the cabin where the boys were awaiting her arrival she asked for grace to deal with the first boy she met. Reaching the porch, she was met by two of them. What she said, she does not remember; but to her amazement one of them immediately responded by saying, "I wish you had spoken to me before. I have been waiting all the week for somebody to talk to me on these things." Joined by two more boys they sat there in the porch in the gathering dusk and talked about the Lord Jesus. How easy it was now she had started! In simple words she explained why He came, and what He does for those who trust in Him. And when she packed them off to their beds she was happy in the knowledge that these four, at least, had heard the Gospel from her lips. At next morning's breakfast table, R. G. himself, having been informed of the events of the previous evening, spoke to the boys, with the result that six received Christ as their Saviour. One of the six became a missionary to South America.

That experience convinced Mrs. LeTourneau of the value of camps, and made her ambitious to found one for herself, where boys and girls could have all the benefits of out-of-doors recreation, coupled with sincere Christian teaching. That ambition had its fulfillment eventually in Bethany Camp, Winona Lake, and in its successors in Arkansas and Texas. Her camps are run by young people for young people. Groups of twelve to fifteen are placed under the care of a Counsellor, whose task it is to preserve discipline, organize games and hold "family" devotions. The Counsellors are usually college students, in which connection Mrs. LeTourneau has enjoyed the co-operation of Wheaton College, Illinois, that great Evangelical training-ground for American youth. In addition to the personal work done by the Counsellors, daily meetings are held for the children, addressed by men and women who are experts in presenting the Gospel to juvenile listeners.

Life certainly has no dull moments for Evelyn Le-Tourneau, with her business responsibilities as a Director of R. G. LeTourneau Incorporated, her camp interests, the ex-G.I.s at Longview to mother, and her home obligations to discharge. What her annual automobile mileage is who could tell? That is something for "Believe-it-or-not" Ripley to work upon. Suffice to say that she is a first-class driver, which is not surprising since she learned her skill from R. G. before she was out of her teens. There is only one thing she likes better than being at the wheel, and that is flying in her husband's plane, for she agrees with him that there is nothing like air travel for "going places quickly".

And now, having told of her many activities for other people's children, it may be appropriate to conclude this chapter with a description of the LeTourneau family circle. After their first disappointment and grief, God gave to Bob and Evelyn five more sons and a daughter. Donald, the eldest boy, was killed in a 'plane accident, as we have already recorded. Following him came Richard, now married (proud father, too, of R. G. the Second) and working in his father's factory at Longview, after service with the U. S. Army in Japan. Next is Roy, recently settled at Longview, following graduation from Wheaton Academy; and the last of the boys are Ted and Benny, who are still at school. The only daughter, Louise, is married to an employee of the LeTourneau company, and has three children of her own. Which just shows how the years go by!

CHAPTER IX

"THE BUMBLEBEE CANNOT FLY"

" ACCORDING to the theory of aerodynamics, and as may be readily demonstrated through laboratory tests and wind-tunnel experiments, the Bumblebee is unable to fly. This is because the size, weight, and shape of his body, in relation to the total wingspread, makes flying impossible.

"But the Bumblebee, being ignorant of these profound scientific truths, goes ahead and flies anyway—and manages to make a little honey every day."

This delightful piece of irony hangs upon the wall of one of the Peoria offices, and there can be no doubt as to who was in the mind of the person who placed it there. Though we hesitate to pursue too far the analogy between R. G. and this Bumblebee, and at once want to substitute the word "defiant" for "ignorant", it nevertheless remains that both persist in doing what wiseacres say cannot be done—and succeed.

With the Bumblebee, of course, it is just crass stupidity that makes him fly in the face of the experts; but with R. G. it was necessity that drove him in the first place to attempt the unorthodox and achieve the impossible. Away back in his Stockton days he wanted new tools and new machines, and simply had not the money to buy them. So he set to work making them for himself. From a pile of scrap steel he took a gear and a pinion and what-not besides, and from these available components built up whatever was required. The result may not always have been elegant, and the engineering aesthete might have curled his lip in scorn; but the designer felt that he could be contemptuous of appearance when his creation not only worked, but did a better job than much of the expensive, burnished and enamelled equipment that was on the market.

An overhead crane was one of his earliest and most urgent requirements, and to buy one of standard design would have involved considerable expense. So he set to work on his own idea of what an overhead crane should be like—and ever since he has been building overhead cranes, and other cranes, too, which for lifting-power and reach have left stereotyped models far behind. Members of the old guard like to recall how, in the early days at Peoria, an unloading crane became an urgent necessity. R. G. sketched his idea on a piece of paper one afternoon, and twenty-four hours later the new piece of equipment was at work! Today, in the Peoria plant, there are two overhead cranes with a span of 100 feet, which have carried as much as 20 tons each. Both were constructed to R. G.'s design and under his supervision. And before we leave this subject of cranes, the great-grandfather of them all must be mentioned. It was built on the bank of the Mississippi at Vicksburg, for unloading material from river barges. This giant is 300 feet long, and can lift 50,000 lbs. without protest, stretching 150 ft. out from the bank of the river to grab its load.

One of the items of equipment to which R. G. turned his personal attention was a press. Once again, shortage of cash was the necessity which mothered invention; and the result was a machine which made the operators jump for joy. They had begun to boast that the boss's gadgets stepped up production fourfold; and this new contribution strengthened their case. So R. G. went on building presses. At Peoria, in 1935, he needed one that would be hydraulically operated, and got busy on his drawing-board. That machine is in operation today, and is in daily use.

So it would be possible to go on. Take lathes as another example. Approaching the need from a purely practical point of view, he produced his own *Tournamatic* lathe, the excellence of which is demonstrated from the large number now in use at every one of the four LeTourneau plants. "For some jobs, no other machine on the market can keep up with it," is the tribute of one of the principal engineers of the company. The way in which it eats up metal needs to be seen to be believed, and it is capable of taking any amount of abuse.

Special presses, forging hammers, drilling and turning machines, furnaces, dies—these and a host of other things have come from his fertile brain, to be built in his own factories, and proved there as to their efficiency and durability. It has in fact been claimed by those qualified to express an opinion that "R. G.

LeTourneau is always ahead of others in the same business. He is in the same class as Edison and Ford. He has more ideas than he will ever get developed. His brain is buzzing with them. What Frank Lloyd Wright has been to architecture, that LeTourneau is to dirt-moving machinery."

One advantage which R. G. enjoys over many others is that he began at the bench and not with the text-book. Thus he actually did many things which after-wards he learned could not be done. These discoveries did not cause him to rank himself as a miracle-worker, but they did produce an ingrained suspicion of theo-reticians. And again and again during his career he has made these gentlemen eat their words by defy-ing their so-called "laws" and producing machines which the experts have declared to be impracticable.

There was an occasion, for example, when he wanted a threading machine to cut a fourfold thread in steel. His own idea was that it should work from a twenty-five horse-power motor, which to perform the required task must reverse fifty times every minute. He called in a firm of carbide tool specialists, who shook their heads, and said: "It can't be done." On all the avail-able information it certainly looked as though R. G. was this time asking too much of any machine. Just figure it out for yourself, and imagine the strain on a motor which had to change its mind—and its direc-tion—fifty times in sixty seconds, while all the time it ploughed a tool through steel! But R. G. believed it could be done, and confounded the specialists by producing the machine himself. What others declared to be "a crazy idea" is now in regular service at Peoria, and shows no sign of betraying the reputation of its designer. He has since developed a motor which will put out fifty horse-power, and will completely reverse itself from full speed (3600 RPM) to full speed in the opposite direction in a quarter second.

Many similar cases could be cited. Once R. G. wanted a hydraulic vertical drill. The experts said he could have it, but it wouldn't be vertical. That was against all engineering practice, and the thing must be horizontal or it would not work. "Very well," was the answer they received, "you say it can't be done, and I say it can, so I'll prove to you that I am right." A few months later the sceptics were invited to visit the plant, and there they saw for themselves in operation the machine which they had pronounced impossible. To give them the credit which is due to them, they took back their words, and asked permission to copy R. G.'s design for their own use.

An almost parallel circumstance arose over an electric motor on which Mr. LeTourneau was working. He had revolutionary ideas about it, and called in some consulting engineers to ask their opinion. They talked for an hour or more, and then declared pontifically that he would be violating the laws of electricity, and must abandon the plan.

"But why not try the thing?" they were asked.

"Because it is against everything that has been written on the subject."

"Surely the idea is worth exploring."

"No, for we should just be wasting our time."

To R. G. this was nothing more than obstinacy and prejudice, and he turned to the engineers with the pointed advice:

"If I were you gentlemen, I would throw away my books, and try the thing out."

But, after all, they *were* consulting engineers, and he was seeking their expert help, so perhaps they could be pardoned for sticking to their point of view. It was just too bad when, about a year later, they received an invitation bearing the Peoria postmark. "Come and see the thing which you said could not be done," it read.

Perhaps none of R. G.'s engineering achievements are more remarkable than his electrical patents. It will be recalled that his initial improvement in land-levelling machinery was by introducing electrical controls, and he has been working on this idea from that day until now.

Those early motors operated by means of long cables, stretching sometimes the whole length of the machine, and resulting in a tremendous loss of power. This leakage of precious energy troubled R. G. until he devised means whereby he could place the motors right on top of the jobs they had to perform. Was power wanted to raise the gate of a scraper? Very well, put a motor there! Was it needed to lift the bowl? Then put another there! This dispensed with gears and clutches and cables all over the place. A small electric button under the driver's hand provided all that was necessary to set the respective motors at their tasks.

These motors themselves represent a tremendous advance on orthodox principles, according to which they should begin to operate at a minimum speed and work up to a maximum. That, however, was useless for heavy duty like raising the bowl of a scraper; so R. G. designed a motor to develop maximum speed in one sixth of a second. He also showed how a fifty-horse-power motor could be built to occupy no more space than a conventional ten-horse-power design.

To change the subject to something of very practical interest—*houses*. Mr. LeTourneau has been interested in building houses ever since he arrived in Peoria and had no accommodation for his workers. With characteristic directness, he decided to provide them himself, and thereafter, whether at Toccoa, Vicksburg, or Longview, he has surrounded his factories with dwellings of his own design and construction.

For some time he remained faithful to steel as the material *par excellence* for prefabricated homes. ("Prefabricated!" That word has an up-to-date ring about it though we are writing of more than twelve years ago. So once again R. G. appears as a pioneer.) Large sections of the Peoria factory itself were constructed from steel units, and it was a natural step to employ the same technique for house construction. The neat little homes clustered around the Georgia plant testify to the soundness of this method.

But R. G. is nothing if not progressive, and he saw

"Engines of War" describing LeTourneau's contribution to the conflict against German, Italian and Japanese world tyranny, is one of the fascinating chapters in this book. This picture was taken at an eastern Air-borne Engineer Training Center.

In the North African campaign, bridges destroyed by the Germans might have held up the Allied advance, had not LeTourneau equipment been available. Here, near the Kasserine Pass, a demolished bridge is being replaced by a causeway of earth. The lower picture shows a bulldozer dealing with war debris in Belgium.

bigger possibilities in concrete. His first experiments were with concrete blocks; but, always ready to try the unconventional, he argued that it was possible to make a mould of giant proportions from which could be cast a complete concrete house. So he set to work and produced several designs in these monolithic dwellings before at last arriving at a method which promises to revolutionize house construction.

Housewives are familiar with the principle of pouring puddings into fancy moulds, the shapes of which are assumed by the puddings once they have set. This is the simple principle behind the *Tournalayer*, except that the "pudding" in this case is hollow. Actually, two moulds are used, an inner and an outer, and between them is poured the concrete, which hardens around steel mesh which has previously been placed in position. When the concrete has set, a mammoth trailer picks up the outer mould, together with the house, and transports it to a selected site, where the trailer deposits its load, and goes off leaving behind what can be recognized as a potential dwelling. Spaces for windows and doors are already there, important details like these not having escaped the designer's mind.

Well, there it is—a machine that "lays" houses! Introduced at a time when the demand for emergency housing was clamant in a score of countries, it was not surprising that the *Tournalayer* became the subject of keen inquiry and investigation, and the name of its inventor acquired new fame. Not less interesting than the *Tournalayer* itself is its auxiliary, the *Tourna-mixer,* a concrete mixer of extraordinary design (it looks like a colossal gun) capable of containing seven yards of concrete, which it can discharge right into the top of the house moulds.

People have said of R. G. LeTourneau that he has "wheels in his head". Certainly, the variety of his brain-children, and their proven value, indicate a mind of great activity, orginality and independence. Altogether he has more than 170 patents to his credit—a number which has constantly to be revised as he thinks up new notions and puts them to work.

Chapter X

ENGINES OF WAR

WHEN, on December 7, 1941, the Japanese treacherously attacked Pearl Harbor, and war leaped overnight from the West to the East, LeTourneau equipment was in the field almost from zero hour. This is how it happened.

Not only the ships in the famous Hawaiian harbor, but also the airfields around, were left a shambles from that unexpected blow. The Master Mechanic on the spot was glad that he had a team of bulldozers to be set to work at once pushing the damaged and destroyed 'planes off the airfields, so that reinforcements might be flown in. But when he had done that he was faced by the fact that among the wreckage was much valuable material, which if promptly salvaged, could be used to hit back.

Being a man of initiative, he turned to his fleet of forty-one *Tournapulls,* and two of these he converted into flexible crane units by removing the scrapers and substituting tractor cranes with *Tournapull* yokes. These did the work with surprising speed and efficiency. They not only untangled the wrecks, sorting them out for salvage, but also raised dismounted guns, remounting them where possible, or, failing that, installing new ones. And they did it as easily as a soldier puts a rifle on his shoulder! When motor trucks ran off the roads in the black-out, these improvised cranes picked them up bodily, and replaced them on the roads without unloading.

One day the cranes were put through their paces before an impressive-looking group of uniformed spectators which included Admiral Chester W. Nimitz. The Master Mechanic claimed that they would lift 30,000 lbs.; but he was under-estimating their powers, for when demonstrated they added to their reputation by lifting 5,000 lbs. above that figure, and doing it with complete nonchalance. Shortly after this, one of the cranes was borrowed by the U. S. Navy, placed on the deck of the *Saratoga,* and driven around to test its maneuverability. Its first working assignment was to lift a 'plane from a gaping hole in the deck made by a Japanese bomb. The crane did its work with distinction, and was forthwith conscripted into the Navy.

The performance of these emergency-built cranes pointed to the possibility of using rubber-tired, quick-maneuverable *Tournacranes* on aircraft carriers to make short work of clearing the decks of crashed and damaged machines, removing them to places where they could be repaired and put back into service. Navy officials described what was needed, and Mr. LeTourneau sat down to his drawing-board to design apparatus which met their requirements.

To say that the result was satisfactory would be an understatement. The fact is that the Army got to know about the Navy's cranes, and called in R. G. to assist them with a similar problem. Could he build a mobile crane capable of picking up the largest bomber in use, and then carry it away? R. G. knew he could; but there was some fun over red tape about blue prints which raised R. G. to white heat before he made the officials understand that he preferred to demonstrate the practicability of his crane in action, and not to have the design criticized and modified in advance by service technicians. The big fellows which he designed, and later manufactured in large numbers, lifted 60,000 lbs. at a distance of 35 feet from their own rear wheels—and then drove off with the great bomber suspended in mid-air. Imagine what this meant on a busy air-strip when a machine crashed and the wreckage had to be cleared away in double-quick time.

The LeTourneau plants in the Middle-West and South were quickly geared to war-time production. When the call came for shells there was a speedy switch-over to this task, and at one time the plants had an output of 40,000 155-mm. shells monthly. In this connection R. G. designed a heavy-duty lathe which was used in the manufacture of these shells, and in addition an improved nosing press, radically faster and more efficient than others, which was employed in the shaping of shell casings. Rough-cutting and quenching tools, band-seat cutting heads, heat-treat ovens, and similar tooling pieces designed by Mr. Le-Tourneau and manufactured in his factories, contributed toward the waging and winning of the war. A cast steel armor-piercing 155-mm. shell, with all the required tooling machinery, likewise originated from the same source.

Of course, turning out shells by the thousand gave LeTourneau employees a good feeling: they were really doing something to help their buddies in the front line. But it was not long before all responsible realized that the very best contribution these factories could make toward the national effort was by concentrating on the manufacture of their peace-time products. This point was well put by Lieut.-Col. C. H. Chorpening, Executive Office, Supply Division, Corps of Engineers, when, writing to Mr. LeTourneau on behalf of the Chief of Engineers, he said:

"A great many manufacturers seem to feel that only when they get on to tanks, 'planes, guns and shells will they be in real war-work. Tanks, 'planes, guns and shells are important, we've got to have them, but—and I can't make this too strong—to carry the fight to the Japs and Nazis we've also got to have plenty of construction equipment.

"Bulldozers and *Carryall* scrapers in the hands of engineer troops are just as important as rifles and machine guns in the hands of the infantry. What's more, bulldozers and scrapers in this war will get just as close to the enemy and be under just as heavy fire in many cases as will tanks and 'planes. Before this war is over you'll hear plenty about how tractors equipped with bulldozers and scrapers cleared the way to bring up heavy guns, dug gun emplacements, repaired bomb and shell craters to keep ammunition and

guns rolling, cut trenches and threw up embankments
to help landing-parties hold beach-heads, and other
similar jobs."

This was certainly a call to "go to it", and R. G.
and his loyal helpers responded with all their will.
Every effective method was called into play to stimulate the workers to greater and greater production.

"A single 'dozer," read one of the company's state-
ments issued to employees, "replaces scores of soldiers
with shovels and picks when digging a gun emplace-
ment, gouging out a trench, building a tank trap, etc.
With rifles and machine-guns those replaced men
greatly increase our fire-power. Developing an invasion beach-head, a LeTourneau crane unloading
supplies cuts out back-breaking hand labor, and enables
the landing party to throw a much heavier stream
of hot lead. On a bombed airport, a single LeTourneau
Carryall and one operator soldier can move more dirt
and move it faster than a hundred soldiers with shovels
and wheelbarrows. Result: our 'planes can get into
the air faster, and we have more soldiers to man anti-
aircraft batteries."

It did not take the LeTourneau staff long to realize
the important part it was called upon to play in the
global struggle, and bulldozers, scrapers, cranes, sheep-
foot rollers and other equipment rolled off the assembly
lines in ever-increasing numbers, to be despatched
to every field of Allied attack. Altogether, the three
factories poured out a wartime total of equipment
valued at 131 million dollars, or approximately 120,000

units. Much of this became standard equipment, or the only machinery of its type used by the U. S. Army, Aviation and Combat Engineers. Special contracts were also filled for the Navy. The figure of 131 million does not include another approximate eight million dollars valued in armor-piercing shot and shell-casings, manufactured so long as Government demand existed.

Faced with these surprising statistics one's mind goes back to the young man with his welding-torch in the Navy Yard at Vallejo, seeking to make his contribution to World War I. Nobody then could foresee the greater holocaust which was to sweep the continents twenty-five years later, or the part which this "one-tool mechanic" would play against German and Japanese aggression, when the machines which had made his name famous throughout America would become equally well-known in North Africa, in Italy, in France, in Germany, in England, as well as in the Frozen North and the islands of the tropical seas.

The war service record of the earth-moving and other gear produced at Peoria and the three Southern factories is truly amazing. There was scarcely a battle area where it did not lend a hand, or a strategic point where it did not make some essential contribution. One employee of the company, on duty with the U. S. Army in the South Pacific, wrote home: "I was in the Munda, New Georgia, campaign, and believe me this is one rough place over here. LeTourneau equipment played its part, keeping roads built behind us so our supplies could come up. Without roads for supplies battles can't be won. Where you see some *Tournapulls* and 'dozers, roads spring up overnight. After the hard battles were over it sure made me homesick to sit and watch *Tournapulls* at work once more."

It needed a world survey in those days to catalogue the places where LeTourneau products were in service. They went to the Aleutian Islands with the U. S. Army Task Force, and helped to build ramps for landing operations. They worked on airfields in Canada, Britain, North Africa, Australia and Hawaii. They levelled ground for barracks in Trinidad; carved roads through steep and stony mountains in India; constructed a strategic coastal highway in South Africa; and prepared runways in New Guinea.

Probably none of the work accomplished was more important than the creation of air-strips. As early as December, 1942, Lieut.-Col. J. W. Donoghue, on an observation trip for the U. S. Army Chief of Engineers, reported: "The key to forward motion in the Pacific Islands against the enemy is the rapid construction of airdromes at advanced points." This meant that earth-moving equipment had to be not only in the front line, but ahead of it, making possible the next leap forward on the part of the airborne units. "Airpower is earth-moving power," were the emphatic words used by Col. H. A. Montgomery, Executive Office, Supply Division, Office of Chief Engineer, who paid a visit to the Peoria plant in 1943. His inspiring message to the staff on that occasion is so much to the point as to be worth recording.

"The fundamental principle back of this new type of warfare," he said, "is that the mobility of an air force hinges on the bulldozers and other earth-moving equipment in the hands of the engineer half of the Engineer Air Force Team. To keep 'em flying we've got to keep the dirt flying! And that is why Le-Tourneau equipment is so vital to us.

"I wish I could have here with me today the crew of a certain B-26 medium bomber, for they could give you a much better idea than I can of what LeTourneau earth-moving equipment meant to them. On a shipping foray over the Mediterranean during the Tunisian campaign they ran into a storm and were lost over the coastal mountains, with their fuel running low. Their pilot-captain gave them a chance to bail out, but they preferred to stick to the ship while he tried to crash land it in the shallow water just off the shore. There was the pilot 'sitting upstairs' waiting for the gas to give out, when the co-pilot tapped him on the shoulder, pointing down. Below them was what he later described as the longest runway he had ever seen in North Africa—and by far the most welcome!

"Two weeks previously that runway did not exist. It was one of a string built by our engineers for the Coastal Command, constructed to give air protection to the port of Bone, most easterly of the Mediterranean ports used by the Allied Forces at that time for shipping supplies direct by water route to the front. It was a 'pay target' for the Axis 'planes—so much so that the decision had been made to close the port unless air protection could be provided against the constant bombing.

"The only area near Bone that could by any stretch of the imagination be called flat was the delta of the Seybouse River, which General Davidson (engineer for the N. W. Africa Air Force) described as 'pure mud eighteen feet deep'. Besides the mud the only building material available was dune sand from the beach, also abundant, but unfortunately across the river from the air field site.

"The general saw one possibility: to get heavy earth-moving equipment over to the sand dunes, and build a sand road to the river, and then a sand causeway *across* the river. Building the sand road and the causeway took five of the allotted fourteen days. In the remaining nine, with every piece of heavy earth-moving equipment in North Africa concentrated on the job, his engineers moved 66,000 cubic yards of sand to form a thick blanket 150 feet wide over the runway length. As fast as the sand was dumped and spread they laid on it a runway surface of steel plank. On the afternoon of the fourteenth day there was a cloudburst; but by then the job was licked. That B-26 was the first satisfied customer. When the pilot got that ship down he didn't have enough gas left to taxi off the runway!"

Even to the expert such a performance appears almost incredible but later in his talk Col. Montgomery related even more remarkable achievements, thanks to LeTourneau aid. "After the Germans had been driven out of the Kasserine Pass," he said, "the commander of five groups of fighters in the Tactical Air Force asked for five new fields closer to his objectives. The five fields were ready for him seventy-two hours after he made his request. Five days later he moved to six more advanced fields prepared at his request. He just ordered his 'planes forward, trusting that the engineers would have a place levelled off for them to land when they had to come down. Even a few hours' delay in finishing that job could have meant the loss of some of those 'planes."

One observer, making a hurried survey of the Allied Forces in North Africa, counted fifty-five airfields in construction at one time. Between November, 1942, and May, 1943, nearly 120 new airfields were put into use there by the Allies, and all of them required the use of heavy earth-moving equipment.

But although this work was of supreme importance to the course of war, other tasks fell to LeTourneau machinery which were scarcely less in importance, and certainly quite as spectacular. There was the Alaska Highway, the building of which has been described as the greatest engineering feat since the construction of the Panama Canal. This 1,670 miles of all-weather highway was intended to link a chain of airfields for the defense of Alaska, the enemy's key to North America, and also to provide a north-west passage along which supplies could flow to Russia, then fighting desperately to stem the Nazi hordes.

"Push a pioneer road to completion with all speed within the physical capacity of the troops." In these urgent terms the orders to begin the road were issued in March, 1942. By the end of the following month eight miles had been completed, and by October 25 of that same year seven engineering regiments, with the help of contractors, had under construction 1,645 miles of passable road. On November 20 the highway was in service. Critics had declared the project crazy. But men and machines pitted their strength and their skill against temperatures which ranged from ninety degrees above to sixty below zero, against mosquitoes, mud, rains, flood, swamps and perpetually frozen terrain, and won through. A splendid road from Dawson Creek, British Columbia, to Fairbanks, Alaska, today declares their triumph.

The most memorable date for those engaged in this mighty undertaking was October 25, 1942, when the 18th Engineers, pushing westward from Whitehorse, met the 97th Engineers working eastward to complete the last lap of the pioneer road. The event was marked by the operators of the leading 'dozers of the two regiments shaking hands across their LeTourneau blades. The manner of that meeting was highly appropriate, for no road owed more in its construction to bulldozers. Ground locating parties, working from aerial photographs, blazed a centre line through the hundreds of miles of forest. A leading bulldozer, following close behind, cleared a swathe along that line. Next came two or four more 'dozers, knocking down trees and pushing debris off to the side. Smaller 'dozers came behind, and drawing up the rear came the culvert and bridge builders, scrapers, graders and other equipment. "When the ground was firm," reported Brig.-Gen. Clarence L. Sturdevant, Assistant-Chief of Engineers, "ten or twelve bulldozers could clear two or three miles through solid forest each day." Not only the Army Engineers, but the contractors also working with them, both on the pioneer road and the main highway, employed LeTourneau gear.

Experience of the Alaska Highway proved invaluable for the next similar task, the construction of the New Burma Road, to which many of the American engineer troops were transferred. Even with modern equipment they faced a formidable proposition, 8,000 miles from home and therefore from replacement parts. "All natural obstacles that ever teamed up to plague a road-builder are present on this new 'Road to Tokyo'," wrote an authority who saw the problem for himself. Clearing the ground was a gigantic job. Mahogany and teakwood trees had literally to be blasted out; but LeTourneau 'dozers were there to pile these giants of the forest after they had fallen, and to make easy work of the smaller trees and jungle growth. After nine months of incredible effort, the first stretch of the road was finished, and new laurels had been won by machines which bore the LeTourneau name.

The full story would require a book to itself, for on every front quick-witted men saw the possibilities of these machines, and used them for purposes of strategic value. When at the Kasserine Pass the Germans attempted to hold up the Allied drive through mid-Tunisia by wrecking railway-bridges, the Texan commander of an engineer battalion looked at one wrecked bridge and said: "We can shoofly that and have trains running in a week." What he meant by "shoofly" is best explained by the operation itself. His idea was to run the railway track round a little knoll, and then over the river by means of a causeway not more than twenty feet above water level, with three or four wooden box culverts to carry whatever water might be running in the river bed for the remainder of the wet season. He put to work three bulldozers and three *Tournapulls*, with a D-7 Pusher. In nine days, in spite of work-delaying rains and an attack by the German air force, the job was done. The battalion, plus one platoon, had relaid 2,800 feet of track through a cut of 500 cubic yards, and had put in over 6,000 cubic yards of earth as fill. Thus, in little over one week, rail connections were restored, against an estimated two or three weeks for orthodox methods.

So equipment which had been designed for peaceful tasks such as grading farms and making roads, became mighty machines of war, and speeded the battle forward until it was possible to assault the enemy's

European citadel. The world waited impatiently for the opening of the "Second Front", and when the vital day dawned, and the flower of British and American youth was poured across the Normandy beaches into France, LeTourneau juggernauts went with them. An observer of D-Day operations wrote: "I wish Mr. LeTourneau could have watched his equipment working on the beach-head at the time of the invasion, doing wonders that one would think impossible. I am sure he would have felt proud in seeing what great work his machines had done."

Proud, indeed, and justifiably so, but let us not fail to give credit where it is due, and remember that fine machines are useless without fine men to operate them —and they had the finest of men in those epic days. Two 'dozer operators received the Distinguished Service Cross (the second highest U. S. Army decoration) for work accomplished under intense enemy fire on D-Day. They worked in shifts with their 'dozer while it was the specific object of intense mortar and cannon fire, and dragged capsized wheeled and track-propelled vehicles out of the surf. With the battle raging about them, they set out in their unprotected 'dozer to clear obstructions from beach exits. This dangerous objective accomplished, they smashed road blocks and filled in gaping anti-tank traps, while geysers of earth from bursting shells rained upon their machines.

We salute such heroes, and that recognition may be given to other similar exploits, we add a British Press correspondent's report from the Volturno front, Italy.

"I saw four American heroes die at the wheels of bulldozers, cutting down a newly-won portion of the north bank of the Volturno River to clear the way for tanks. Only a few minutes after the first bulldozer went to work the driver was blown to pieces by a German shell. A second man climbed into the seat. A German shell blew up both him and the bulldozer. Within a half-hour, two more bulldozers and their drivers were knocked out. The last was hit just as he pushed aside the last lump of earth barring the bank to tanks."

By-and-by, when the bloodshedding was over, there were devastated cities to clear of the debris of war as a first step toward reconstruction. Here was a task for which bulldozers and scrapers and cranes were surely born; and wherever they were wanted they were there. Londoners saw them make short work of rubble, wood and stone from bomb-damaged buildings. People of France accepted their help in clearing and rebuilding railways. In Holland, the return to normality was speeded as these many-purpose machines disposed of the lumber of war. And in Germany itself the victorious Allies put them to work removing everything that impeded their progress.

Such, in brief outline, was the contribution made by R. G. LeTourneau and his colleagues, at desk and at lathe, to the winning of the war. And when the bugles sounded for peace, new ideas for tank transport, for sweeping land-mines, and for other war-time purposes were either on R. G.'s drawing-board or in process of construction. No longer wanted, they were put aside and the LeTourneau factories, with a minimum of reorganization, turned from producing engines of war to the happier tasks of peace.

CHAPTER XI

MASTER AND MEN

THERE have been prominent industrialists who have professed to be Christians, but who have scrupulously avoided mixing religion and business. It is difficult to understand how such segregation of interests can be reconciled with Christ's all-inclusive claims, or how, indeed, it is possible to practice Christianity at all on a part-time basis. Certainly R. G. LeTourneau knew from the first that to acknowledge the lordship of Christ meant to acknowledge it in everything. He must not only be a respectable citizen, a loving husband, and a good father, but he must also be an exemplary employer, his business relationships being worthy of his profession. In short, he must be "God's business man", demonstrating before a cynical and incredulous world the possibility of maintaining Christian standards in the rough-and-tumble of modern commercial life.

To say as much may be to invite criticism. Doubtless there have been incidents in his life (R. G. would be the first to admit it) when these high ideals have not been fully realized. Probably there are folk who feel that, in their case, less than justice has been received at the hands of the company which bears the LeTourneau name (incidentally, it is inevitable that a man should be blamed for the actions of his representatives, although he may not actually be responsible). But these lapses are only noticeable because of the contrast they afford with general practice. In a business run upon hard, commercial lines, staff dissatisfactions may be so common as to be taken for granted, and not remarked upon. But when a man "sticks his neck out" by a public, nation-wide testimony to his Christian discipleship, it is the easiest thing in the world to find a few bricks to throw at him.

The principles of staff relationship which operate in R. G. LeTourneau Inc. were not worked out in board meetings, but are the expression of R. G.'s own character and convictions. Take, as an example, the unique democratic spirit which prevails throughout the company. If it had been artificially created it might have degenerated to the ludicrous, and resulted in disorganization and indiscipline. But because it is the expression of R. G.'s own personality, and a natural development in the circle which has grown around him, therefore it is successful and makes for harmony and comradeship, which in turn have their influence upon production.

Go back to Stockton, and watch that little group who laid the foundations of this business! Their relationships were based upon the common interests, aspirations, anxieties, achievements, pleasantries and familiarities of a family. Bob was like a father to them all, and Evelyn their mother. There was no question as to who was boss, but there was nevertheless a partnership of effort in which no task was avoided for its difficulty or despised because of its unimportance. If Bob was willing to take his share of the dirty work (and he was!), and even Evelyn would leave her kitchen to run urgent errands (which she often did!), there was no room to be slack or choosey or superior. They were brothers in endeavor.

And there is this further important point. Many of the boys were believers, and some came to know Jesus Christ as their Saviour through the testimony of Bob and Evelyn, and when that happened the distinction between employer and employed was abandoned for the intimacies of Christian fellowship. Most, if not all of them, transferred to Peoria when the new beginning was made there in 1935, and formed the nucleus around which the business grew. Was it not inevitable that the happy informality of their association should set the tone for the future?

Today, it is impossible for R. G. to know all his employees by name, as he did when his pay-roll could be carried around in his own pocket-book, but by example and by precept he encourages his managers to cultivate the same friendliness. He has no use for the officious, bossy spirit, or for managerial airs. For this reason, he believes in one canteen for all his workers, from executives to office boys; and when dinner-time comes he takes his place in the cafeteria queue, selects and pays for his meal, and carries it to the table, which as likely as not he will share with mechanics or clerks.

As will be realized, this means that R. G., instead
of being confined behind the glass partitions of a
presidential office, moves freely among his staff, and
is accessible to all of them. There is no outer ring
of secretaries or inner ring of executives to be penetrated before a matter can be brought to his personal
attention. Walking the corridors with his hat upon
the back of his head, or eating his meals in the cafeteria, he is an easy target for criticism or complaint
or suggestion.

One question inevitably arises in view of Mr. Le-
Tourneau's Christian convictions: Does he insist upon
a profession of Christian faith on the part of those
who seek employment with his company? Point is
given to the inquiry when it is discovered how large
a proportion of the men and women about him in his
business departments are avowed believers and active
church-members. As it was once remarked: "You
have to be careful what you say at LeTourneau's, for
the man you are speaking to may be a Christian!"

There was an occasion when this matter was referred to R. G. himself. His prompt reply was: "No,
all my people are not Christians. And if they were,
I should bring in some who were not, to give the
Christians material to work on!" No applicant for
employment is asked whether or not he has religious
convictions, or, if he has, what their character may
be. The sole qualification for inclusion in the pay-
roll is ability to do the job that is required. Of course,
there is no knowing what may happen *after* a person

has joined the staff. Before the last page of this book has been turned, stories will have been related of those who signed on as unbelievers or as nominal Christians, and who, at their place of business, entered into an experience of Jesus Christ which has transformed their lives.

What, then, about the employment of relations? R. G. has strong opinions on this subject. He is fond of telling about an incident in his life when he was in partnership, and the partner complained about the large number of members of the LeTourneau family who were on the job. "The trouble was," says R. G. with one of his broad smiles, "that there *were* a lot of my family on the job. I haven't any objection to employing relations—*provided you make them work!*"

That principle is carried out without regard to the closeness of kinship of those who join the company. Some well-intentioned fathers regard it as their duty to provide their sons with safe and easy positions, appointing them to arm-chair directorates almost from school. Not so R. G. Each of his boys has in turn gone into the business, but has had to begin at the bottom, knowing that his future position would entirely depend upon the way in which he acquitted himself. It is doubtful whether such an understanding has ever been expressed in words, but everybody who knows R. G. knows that his test for machines and men is identical: "Will it do the job well?" And he is as generous with his praise for the man who passes that test, as he is delighted with the efficient machine.

R. G. believes that one of the marks of a good employer is to encourage the ambition of his workers, and to provide them with facilities for self-advancement. Supposing a book-keeper aspires to become an accountant. The company is prepared to pay up to fifty per cent of the fees for special tuition, after a first diploma has been obtained, to enable such a person to qualify for the better job. In all departments the policy is to reward efficiency by promotion, so that a man may climb from a subordinate position to managerial responsibility within the organization. Incentives to aim high are provided in the personal stories of many who now hold executive office but who began as subordinates, and supremely in the career of Mr. LeTourneau himself.

Arising out of this is the company's Suggestion System. Members of the staff having ideas which they believe would improve production or make for greater efficiency are invited to submit them on forms provided for the purpose. If the idea is adopted and results in economy of time or material, with consequent saving of costs, ten per cent of the estimated gross benefit for one year is payable to the originator. Other rewards, ranging from five to one hundred dollars, are payable for accepted suggestions on sales promotion, safety measures, public relations, and other matters.

It is not claimed, of course, that all of these facilities are peculiar to R. G. LeTourneau Inc. Many are practiced in common with American industry as a whole. Most firms of similar size have their group insurance schemes, retirement annuity programs, hospitalization plans, and so forth. The advantage enjoyed by LeTourneau employees is that these are operated on terms which seek to give the maximum benefits; it is a case of going the second mile.

Every encouragement is given to self-help and the realization of legitimate aspirations on the part of members of the staff. For example, a branch of the Federal Credit Union operates at each of the plants, under the approval and sponsorship of the management, which bears certain expenses involved in their conduct. Members of the Union (any employee is qualified for membership, upon payment of a fee of twenty-five cents) may deposit money upon which interest is paid, or may borrow money within reasonable securities. Loans are advanced for domestic emergencies, furniture, and in some cases for cars.

Each factory has an Employees' Activities Association, none of which is entirely self-supporting, so that the company is able to demonstrate its interest in the social pursuits of the staffs by contributions of one kind or another. These Associations organize and foster sports, hobbies, and musical talent, thus helping to promote a spirit of good fellowship. At Toccoa, a well-equipped sports center is provided through the Activities Association, the existence of which calls for the explanation that the Industrial Relationship program varies from plant to plant, each being directed by a local executive who adapts his program according to prevailing circumstances. The Toccoa plant having created its own community, it was obviously necessary to cater in a more thorough manner to the social life of employees. Hence we find either in or around the factory a post office, a clinic staffed by Christian doctors, a grocery and meat store and an automobile service station, all provided by the company. In addition there is the Louise Dairy, which not only supplies good milk but (and this is the testimony of experience) the most delicious ice-cream. The Dairy is now independently operated.

In some matters the Toccoa staff might be considered the most fortunate of all LeTourneau employees, for a whole range of interests and recreations are provided for, thanks to the development of the area since the advent of R. G. There are boating and bathing to be enjoyed in the warm waters of Lake Louise, while the fisherman can always cast his line there in confidence of a good catch. Around the shores of the lake are facilities for picnics, with tables, barbecue pits, running water and electric lights, so that full advantage may be taken of the delightful evenings. "Where else than here," it has been asked, "can an industrial worker have for the shooting or the hooking quail, grouse, rabbit, squirrels, opossum, fox and fish in season?"

Having arrived in the Deep South, it is appropriate to mention the effect upon life, thought and custom of the introduction of heavy industry to areas which had never before produced much more than cotton. It

must be admitted that the reception given to Mr.
LeTourneau was mixed, particularly in Mississippi.
There were progressives who welcomed the coming
of the factories. They had been long concerned over
a condition of depression which resulted, for example,
in the majority of Mississippi college graduates leaving
the State to find employment. But there was also a
reactionary element which was satisfied with things
as they were, and showed alarm at the advent of a
big manufacturer, whose methods (it was supposed)
would conflict with Southern traditions.

Certainly, the opening of these plants brought
problems for R. G. and his management. The first
difficulty was the shortage of supervisory personnel.
Close upon the opening of the Georgia factory came
war, and the Mississippi venture was begun under
conditions of national mobilization. This meant that
skilled men could not be spared from other places, so
there was no alternative to building a staff from
agricultural and semi-skilled hands. Not least of the
difficulties was to overcome the idea that heavy work
was not for white men but should be left to negroes.
And, of course, there were those who were ready
enough to suggest that to employ a colored man in a
factory at all, whatever the duties allotted to him,
was to put dangerous notions into his head.

This is not the place for discussing the Negro problem, described by Cecil Roberts as "the American
headache". We all know the rights and wrongs of it
(or think we do), and many are ardent reformers

from a distance. Neat theories on how to solve the
problem are liable to become frayed and untidy, however, upon first-hand contact with it. As John Gunther
confesses: "I had no conception at all of the grim
enormousness of the problem. The phrase is trite,
but I know of no other: the Negro in the South has to
be seen to be believed." By way of comment it may
be mentioned that in choosing Vicksburg for the site of
his Mississippi factory, R. G. entered an area where
the colored population is fifty-six per cent of the whole.

An industrialist invading the South finds himself at
once up against all the antipathies, prejudices and
passions which this question inflames. He would
quickly make his position impossible if he ignored
them, or if he approached them with the reforming
zeal of the crusader.

The principle of employment in LeTourneau factories in the South is that local tradition as to the relations between white and colored are not violated, thus
ensuring harmony among the workers, and giving
offense to none. But in social amenities the colored
employee enjoys the same advantages as the white.
The effect is seen in their homes, and in their improved ideas of health and sanitation. Moreover,
being in receipt of steady wages they are able considerably to improve their living conditions.

By and large, the coming of the LeTourneau company has resulted in many benefits to the community,
both white and colored. Such items as the provision
of buses to convey employees to and from work, the

institution of sick and holiday pay, and the availability of medical facilities may not impress the reader who is familiar with industrial methods elsewhere; but in the South these things are new and unusual, and their introduction has established a standard which may become the norm of the future.

Upon the wall of R. G.'s Vicksburg office there hangs a declaration which expresses the appreciation of the people of the State of Mississippi. It reads thus, and is signed by the Governor and the Adjutant-General Chief of Staff:

"Know ye, that reposing special trust and confidence, as well in your patriotism as in your integrity and readiness to do good service to the State, I, Thomas L. Bailey, Governor of the State of Mississippi, by virtue of the power and authority vested in me by law, have appointed and constituted you, Robert G. LeTourneau, as Colonel and Aide-de-Camp Governor's Staff, to rank as such from the 18th day of January, A. D. 1944."

It is not always easy to steer a course between the "paternal" attitude in industrial relations, which seeks in a benevolent way to impose its will upon employees, and a genuine solicitude for their welfare. When, as with R. G. LeTourneau, there is added to his realized obligations as employer a deep sense of spiritual responsibility, then the dividing line may appear to some to be finely drawn. How he discharges his Christian duty toward the men and women working for him, without any incursion upon their rights or intrusion upon their personalities, is a story we have yet to tell; but before concluding this chapter it is relevant to mention that his interest in his staff extends beyond them to their children.

Not the least attractive expression of this interest is the annual award of scholarships to leading Christian schools in the United States, including the Moody Bible Institute and Wheaton College, for which junior employees and the sons and daughters of employees may compete. The scholarships provide free tuition, plus twenty-five dollars a month for expenses, over a period of one to four years, according to the qualifications and needs of the candidate. Selection is made at each factory by a board consisting of a Christian minister, an educationalist and a businessman.

It will be realized that R. G.'s program for good industrial relations is not only the application of Christian principles, but also the introduction of the Christian Gospel. Let us hear what he says on this subject, in an address which he has given up and down the country:

"In mechanics our worst enemy is friction. It is that which causes all the trouble. I'm a mechanic; all I know is machinery. I live it, day in, day out. I like powerful machinery—and I like a powerful Gospel. I wish I knew as much about the laws of friction between men as I do about the coefficient of friction of the different materials.

"The most efficient engine we have today, the Diesel motor, converts only about one-third of its potential power into mechanical energy. Two-thirds is wasted. Your automobile doesn't do more than half as well— it gives only one-sixth of its potential—and a lot more is lost in transmitting the power to the wheels. Friction is responsible. The railroad steam engine is even worse. Only about one-sixteenth of the potential power of the fuel it consumes is transformed into mechanical power. The other fifteen-sixteenths goes to waste.

"Wherever you go, on land, on sea, or in the air, there's friction. Boats don't go through water without friction. Planes don't travel the air-lanes without friction. When you go up in the air 10,000 to 15,000 feet you travel ten or fifteen miles an hour faster than at lower levels. That is because there is less friction.

"In a war plant I have watched a hydraulic press, with a 500 horse-power motor to pump the liquid that makes it travel, pierce 155-mm. shells two a minute, and have heard the manager say: 'If I had a bigger motor I could pierce them faster.' For our Vicksburg plant we have designed, built and installed a machine to do exactly the same job as fast or faster, and that machine has only a 200 horse-power motor. So it is fifteen times more efficient. What is the difference? We have reduced friction. That comparison illustrates the damage, trouble and inefficiency that friction causes.

"Mechanical friction is bad. But human friction is worse—friction between man and man. The friction, the touchiness, the hate that is in this old world today! Friction in the home probably is the bitterest of all friction in human relationships. Friction between communities is certainly unpleasant, and friction between nations causes wars that cost thousands of human lives, and disrupts the political, social, economic and moral structure.

"But troublesome as is friction in machinery, bad as is friction between man and man, there is a third type of friction that is far, far worse. The most terrible, the most disastrous, the most tragic friction of all is between God and man. Friction between God and man is the root of the difficulty. If I could eliminate that friction, I could eliminate friction between man and man. If men could only grasp God's plan for eliminating friction between a Holy God and His sinful creatures, we would have little trouble getting rid of friction between men.

"You may set up for yourself a high standard of morals. You may resolve to be unselfish. You may work out for yourself an excellent code of ethics. But the only way to solve the problems of this world is to let God work out His plan for each of our lives, and daily ask Him to lead us. In other words— eliminate the friction. Be willing to be led. And the Christ of Calvary, who paid the price of redemption on the cross, who cried: 'It is finished!' as the veil of the temple was rent from top to bottom, opening the way for us to receive forgiveness and come boldly to the Throne of Grace, He, the Son of God, will dwell in our hearts to give us the power to do what

In the hills of North Georgia, Mr. LeTourneau has created a lake, and built the Lake Louise Hotel beside it. It is an all-steel structure, shaped like a star, with an auditorium seating 1,700 at the centre. The designer was Mrs. LeTourneau.

Interior of Mr. LeTourneau's latest plant, at Longview, Texas. This fine modern factory is 1000 feet long. The center span measures 112 feet and the total width is 312 feet. Here students of the LeTourneau Technical Institute receive their practical training.

we cannot do in our own strength. He will thus bring to an end the friction between God and us, and also between us and our fellow men."

There speaks one who believes that the differences that divide men and occasion strife between them have fundamentally a theological explanation and solution, and that the disturbed harmonies of human relationship need adjustment on two levels, the higher taking precedence of the lower, since there must be reconciliation with God before there can be real cooperation between men. And in the kingdom which he rules he is seeking to demonstrate the truths which he believes.

CHAPTER XII

LEARNING BY DOING

CALEB LETOURNEAU had one outstanding regret—his lack of education, a regret which was all the more acute when he remembered that his father had purposed to make him the scholar, until his brother Joshua lost his arm in a sawmill, and being thereby incapacitated for farm work, took his place at college. "So long as I have a red cent, my kids shall go to college," he used to declare, by way of resolving that none of his children should be handicapped for want of opportunity.

However excellent his intentions, however, Caleb spent very few red cents on the education of Robert, which was entirely Robert's fault, of course, since that wilful youth saw little use for school, and would allow nobody to rest until he had left schooldays behind and gone out into the world in search of a job. Thus he belongs to that distinguished group, which includes many of the outstanding men of our day, whose academic attainments gave little promise of their subsequent successes, and whose contradictory records are frequently quoted to the satisfaction of innumerable little boys and the confusion of their teachers.

It is necessary to emphasize, nevertheless, that Robert's dislike of school did not arise from indolence but from excess of energy, and that when he entered industry and related learning to doing he became

146

greedy for knowledge, and eagerly availed himself of every opportunity to increase it. Being of naturally quick intelligence, he learned as he worked, his keen mind not only readily grasping methods, but probing behind methods to the whys and the wherefores of every process, so that he had an appreciation of the reasons for doing things in certain ways. This was but the first step toward discovering improved methods, for as he argued things out in his mind he was frequently made to realize the possibility of alternatives, which he lost no time in testing, either to discard them as impracticable, or to adopt them in the face of orthodox objection.

His pursuit of knowledge, however, was not altogether independent of outside aid, for he acknowledges his indebtedness to correspondence courses, through which he mastered many of the intricacies of electrical engineering and related subjects, and furnished himself with a fund of basic information which enabled him to launch out into experimental research, the results of which have often routed the experts.

R. G. is too wise to reject text-books as unimportant, but as a result of his own experience he believes in reading them at the bench, where their theories may be tested, and not in the arm-chair, where all their pronouncements are liable to be accepted as final. Hence, his advice to every young man aspiring to engineering attainments is to combine the practical and the technical. But let us listen to him expounding this point himself.

"If a student knows a thing can't be done, naturally he won't try to do it. But why does he know it can't be done? Because the book says so. And too often the reason why the book says so is because some scientist (?) has evolved a theory to explain a certain observed phenomenon. By the time that theory gets to the student in a book it has become, instead of a theory, an assertively proven fact.

"There is on the one hand the danger of knowing too much, being certain something can't be done because some theorist has proven to his satisfaction it can't. And on the other hand there is the handicap of ignorance, thinking that to be feasible which violates natural law. That is why I say practical and technical education should go hand in hand. The so-called practical man without book knowledge is unqualified as an inventor, unbalanced. But the technical man without practical experience is just as unbalanced, unqualified."

Possessing such strong opinions, of course, makes R. G. critical of certain educational methods, as it also makes him critical of those who reject all method. Much orthodox schooling, he believes, has little practical value, hence many high school and college graduates enter the industrial world poorly equipped. But, at the same time, there are individuals who by-pass formal education by going to work at an early age, and find themselves handicapped all through life because of the lack of grounding in fundamentals.

As his staff increased, Mr. LeTourneau saw the

possibility and desirability of giving expression to
his educational philosophy. A start was made at
Peoria in 1937, when home-study courses in elementary mathematics were introduced. There was a ready
response on the part of employees, and the curriculum
was elaborated to meet the wishes of students. By
the end of 1940 over 1,500 certificates had been issued
for completed courses in mathematics, blue-print reading, machine-tool operation, flame-cutting, arc-welding,
and leadership. Additional subjects were added when
ten or more members of the staff signified their
desire for particular studies. Each subject required
the attendance of the student for three hours on two
nights each week, the full course covering ten weeks.
Foremen and specialized workmen provided the training, and all courses were open to the general public.

This pioneering move abundantly justified itself,
and in due course the classes were transferred from
the factory to local schools, under the official education
authority. The looming certainty of war made it all
the more important that engineering workers should
be as highly skilled as possible, and with this as an
impetus, considerable developments were made in the
scheme. At one time as many as seventy per cent
of the staff were under instruction on one or more
subjects. Today, the Peoria Plant has no educational
scheme of its own in operation, but employees are
encouraged to avail themselves of the excellent facilities now provided by the State Department for Education.

Meanwhile, a new beginning had been made at Toccoa, to which Georgian town, it will be recalled, R. G. had been attracted because of the school already operated there by Dr. R. A. Forrest. It was the prospect of enabling mountain boys to combine practical and technical tuition that induced R. G. to establish a factory there. Carrying his educational ideas a step further, he set up schools for welders and machinists, for which youths from eighteen to twenty-one were selected and enrolled. The program provided not only for a limited amount of class room instruction, the two principal subjects being blue-print reading and shop mathematics, but also for fully eight hours daily in practical employment in the plant itself. Many excellent results were obtained from the Toccoa experiment, and the products of the school are today efficient members of either the LeTourneau Company or other similar organizations throughout the States.

The war-time inauguration of the Vicksburg plant made any similar project there impossible; but with the passing of the years an ambition developed in R. G.'s mind for a technical school on a larger scale than anything attempted before. "There have never been enough good mechanics" was an opinion which he frequently expressed; and he hoped—and watched —for an opportunity to establish an institution which would produce men "who not only know how to operate machines, but know all the answers as well".

How that opportunity came is one of the big stories

of his life. To meet the emergencies of war, the
United States Government erected in various parts
of the country large temporary hospitals, where the
wounded from many fields of military engagement
could be brought for healing and recovery. One of
these was sited just beyond the city boundary of
Longview, East Texas. Known as the Harmon General
Hospital, it cost over five million dollars for the land
and buildings alone.

With the war over, this and other similar hospitals
being no longer needed, the question of their disposal
came to the fore, and there was no lack of suggestions
or of applicants for the various properties. It became
a matter of considerable local concern in Longview
what should happen to the Harmon General Hospital,
and a leading citizen and newspaper proprietor, Commander Carl Estes, advanced the proposal that it
should be offered to R. G. LeTourneau to become an
engineering school for the training of American ex-
servicemen. It was mainly due to Commander Estes'
vigorous sponsorship of this scheme that the property
passed into the hands of Mr. LeTourneau early in
1946.

The campus consists of 156 acres in all, covered
by 232 buildings, most being of semi-permanent construction, and nearly all being connected by enclosed
ramps. Besides the many wards, which were easily
adaptable as dormitories or classrooms, or transformed
into comfortable homes for married students and their
families, the hospital area includes many larger struc-

tures which were originally used for social activities. Among other useful installations were a swimming pool and tennis courts, all of which admirably qualified the place for its new purpose. The complete property was assessed for sale at $870,000, and was sold to the LeTourneau Foundation at that figure—less 100 per cent discount! It has to be added, however, that although the initial purchase was negotiated upon such satisfactory terms, considerable expense has been involved in adapting the various buildings for their new use, and in purchasing necessary furnishings and equipment. R. G. also secured the option on an adjoining 10,000 acres of land, upon which to place his newest factory, which measures 310 by 1,000 feet, with plenty of room left for experimental purposes in the development of equipment, for farming, and other uses.

The primary condition of this transaction was that ex-G. I.s should be priority students of the LeTourneau Technical Institute of Texas as long as there was need, and of the 350 students who were in residence in the summer of 1947[1] practically all were in this category. Of this number, 200 had their families with them, and were living on the campus, and their fifty-five children (by no means a static quantity) contributed to the community sense. By using the available accommodations it would be possible to increase the student body to as many as 1,000, and even higher.

[1]The number of students was increased by 200 by the Spring of 1948.

The great advantage which students of the Le-Tourneau "Tech" enjoy over others is provided by the adjacent factory, in which they are not only able to gain practical experience, but are also able to earn dollars in exchange for the service they render. Moreover, the machines and tools which they operate are the latest of their types, which can rarely be claimed for the equipment of the average vocational school. Some 169 welding machines and 391 machine tools are available for practice and performance, the latter ranging from sensitive drills to boring mills valued at $50,000 apiece. The variety of work possible on these machines provides an almost ideal learning situation for the student.

It is possible to think of Mr. LeTourneau, then, as one who is making a substantial contribution to the industrial training of the youth of the United States, and as a pioneer in vocational education. In view of his personal attainments, together with this practical interest in the advancement of others, it is not surprising that several seats of learning should have conferred honorary degrees upon him. He is a Doctor of Science and a Doctor of Law, and has in addition a distinction in Mechanical Engineering. But he carries these honors lightly, and does not allow the esteem of others to rob him of his humility, or, indeed, of his sense of humor.

Mr. LeTourneau was attending the graduation exercises of the Winona Lake School of Theology, Indiana, of which he is a Director. The function was being held in the commodious Billy Sunday Tabernacle and was attended by a large crowd, including many notables. In deference to the occasion, academic robes were worn, and an appropriate dignity was observed.

Mr. Homer Rodeheaver, the celebrated Gospel singer and composer, introduced Mr. LeTourneau, remarking with truth that he was a preacher who had not been through a theological college. Dr. Palmer Muntz, Director of the Winona Lake Conference, added the comment that the speaker of the day was not lacking academic qualifications, but was "several times a doctor". These pleasantries were capped by Doctor LeTourneau himself, when he introduced his address by the words: "I don't let them call me 'Doctor' for fear I might get mixed up with these preachers." After that sally, he proceeded with his message.

But he had not got far when he felt something bite him in the arm—that, at least, is how it felt to him. He tried to ignore it, but the performance was repeated, until at last his hand stole into the wide sleeve of his gown, and closed upon—a wire clothes-hanger! He shifted the thing in the hope that it would cease to discomfort him; but alas! it was not to be pacified. Every time he moved his arm the hanger returned to the attack, and at last R. G. decided that there was nothing for it but to rid himself of his tormentor. His audience was immensely amused when, boldly thrusting his hand into his sleeve, he produced the offending article, exclaiming at the same time: "Doctor or no doctor, there is something wrong with this gown!"

Chapter XIII

MILLIONS FOR GOD

CARLTON CASE, friend and legal adviser to R. G. LeTourneau, looked worried. "Bob," he was saying, "you surely do not appreciate the meaning of this word. It is not my business, even though I am your attorney, to dissuade you and Mrs. LeTourneau from giving your personal wealth for the promotion of Christian work, if that is your wish; but I do consider it my duty to point out the serious implications of this word 'irrevocable'. If you allow it to stand, it means that . . ."

"That I can't take it back again, even if I want to," broke in Mr. LeTourneau himself. "That if an emergency arises, and I am short of money, I cannot dip my hand into this fund. That my children will have no claim upon it. I know all that, but all the same, that word 'irrevocable' has to stand. Do you think that my wife and I want to give this to the Lord today, and take it back again tomorrow?"

Such a question left even the agile mind of the lawyer without an answer. He had become accustomed to the considerable gifts made by Mr. and Mrs. LeTourneau to evangelistic and missionary enterprises, but this latest idea of theirs, involving the signing away of ninety-eight per cent of their means, bewildered him. Their insistence that they realized the implications of what they were doing did not remove his misgivings. That word "irrevocable"! It worried him. He disliked a document which left no loophole for escape. However, he had done his best to expunge the offending word, and had failed. The deed must be signed and sealed as it stood, in terms of the unqualified surrender of a substantial fortune for the service of God.

Thus there came into being, in the year 1935, the "LeTourneau Foundation", described as "a not-for-profit corporation whose income and capital can be used only for the Cause of Christ". The precise purpose and scope of the Foundation is stated as follows:

> "To teach, promulgate and disseminate the Gospel of Jesus Christ throughout the world, and also to unite in Christian fellowship the large number of consecrated Christians in the various Evangelical Churches, and for such purpose to appoint and engage ministers, evangelists, missionaries and others to actively pursue and accomplish the foregoing purposes."

In May, 1947, the Foundation was valued at seven million dollars. It is the largest shareholder in R. G. LeTourneau, Incorporated, holding 63.1 per cent of the common stock. It is the twelfth largest trust in the United States, and the largest religious foundation in this country, and possibly in the world. Since it was formed it has contributed to other organizations engaged in Gospel work over two-and-a-half million dollars, and in addition has directly spent approximately $2,351,601 in carrying out its own program of evangelistic ministries.

Already in the development of this story reference has been made to some of the enterprises which are either owned or maintained by the Foundation, as, for example, the LeTourneau Technical Institute of Texas, the Gospel Radio Station at Toccoa, Georgia, and the Missionary Flying School at the same place. Many other agencies depend for their entire support upon the Foundation, and a growing number of Christian causes in all parts of the world have benefited from its funds.

Soon after its initiation, the Foundation began to sponsor the publication and circulation of Gospel literature. It happened this way. There came to Peoria in 1936 a new member of the company's advertising department, a keen Christian man who believed in the ministry of the printed page. He was editor of a four-page evangelistic leaflet, with the title of *Now,* the distinctive feature of which was that it used items of current news as a vehicle for presenting the Gospel message. Eager to get his publication into as many hands as possible, he asked permission to distribute it among the LeTourneau staff. When the request was referred to the President of the company, he replied that he welcomed the idea, and was willing to print a Peoria edition of *Now* in the company's own printing plant.

That first printing ran to 1,000 copies, which were more than enough for the staff at Peoria and Stockton. But before long the number had to be increased, for employees were beginning to ask for extra copies to give or send to their friends. Then requests from other sources made a mailing list necessary, and the circulation began to mount. At the end of two years 10,000 copies were being put through the press, a number that was more than doubled by the end of the next twelve months, and it has gone on increasing until a recent printing ran to 365,000 copies. This amazing growth in circulation is largely the result of Mr. Le-Tourneau's week-end speaking ministry, from which he never returns without a new batch of names to be added to the mailing list. Today, *Now* has readers in all parts of the world. Of the maximum printing mentioned above, 308,000 were sent to individual readers, and 57,000 in varying quantities for bulk distribution.

Started as a house magazine, *Now* retains a number of features which are mainly of interest to LeTourneau employees, but its wider appeal is ensured by editorials by Mr. LeTourneau himself, articles on topical themes, and a regular page contributed by Tom M. Olson, who has a unique gift for taking news of the day and giving it a Gospel application.

This co-operation with Mr. Olson, who is married to Mr. LeTourneau's sister Marie, opened up another channel of service for the Foundation. Mr. Olson had been a prolific tract writer for many years, and in 1937 the office of *Now* took over responsibility for printing and circulating these. When he began writing for *Now* many of his articles were reprinted as tracts, and mailed to Christian workers far and near. For several years past the number of tracts printed and issued by the Foundation has totalled thirty-three million, and these have carried their message in seven

or eight different languages. Only a small proportion
of these is used by evangelistic agencies immediately
associated with the Foundation, the majority being
gratuitously issued to applicants through the mail.
Not only individual tract distributors, but missionary
societies and other organizations throughout the world
receive generous supplies free of all charge.[1]

It was not long before the growth of evangelistic
activities sponsored by the Foundation suggested the
necessity for appointing a co-ordinating director, under
whose supervision these various interests might be
developed to the best advantage. Another matter calling for attention at the same time was Mr. LeTourneau's schedule of speaking engagements. Requests
for his services were pouring in from all parts of the
United States and from Canada, and it was clearly
important that somebody should be given the task of
dealing with these requests and promoting Mr. Le-
Tourneau's testimony in a businesslike way.

Among those who knew of this need was Dr. J.
Palmer Muntz, pastor of Cazenovia Park Baptist
Church, Buffalo, and director of the Winona Lake
Bible Conference, of which Mr. LeTourneau is president. He was convinced that he knew the very man
for this task—Dr. Harold Strathearn, English by birth,
trained in evangelism in Dr. Samuel Chadwick's Cliff

[1]Figures for 1947 are forty-seven million tracts issued in
English, German, Italian, French, Russian, Ukrainian, Portu-
guese, Spanish, Japanese, Dutch, Tagolog, Creole and Greek.
New tracts are in production in Chinese, Korean, Hungarian,
Bulgarian, Norwegian, Czechoslovakian, Guarani, Cebrian,
Swedish, Marathi, Arabic and other languages.

College, and well experienced in American methods by pastorates in this country followed by executive office as founder and director of the Interstate Evangelistic Association.

A meeting between Mr. LeTourneau and Dr. Strathearn was quickly followed by the latter's appointment, a step which has been abundantly justified by the results. From his office, Dr. Strathearn is able to maintain intimate contact with currents of Christian thought and activity throughout America and the world, and to promote Mr. LeTourneau's personal testimony in a way which ensures its maximum effectiveness. He often accompanies R. G. to his week-end engagements, and when he does so he invariably takes with him his wife, Mrs. Dorothy Strathearn, "The Gospel Nightingale", whose beautiful singing provides a valuable contribution to the meetings.

The LeTourneau Evangelistic Center, as Dr. Strathearn's department is called, has assumed responsibility for a large number of activities sponsored by the Foundation. There are, for example, Bible Camps in various parts of the country, where opportunity is afforded to hear prominent Christian leaders and Bible teachers, and where thousands of young people are brought under the influence of missionary advocates, as well as being grounded in the fundamentals of the Faith. The organizing of Evangelistic Forums is another important function, at which ministers may hear outstanding Christian workers speak of their methods and experiences.

When the U.S. Army Airforce asked for a crane capable of lifting the biggest bombers, this was LeTourneau's answer. With cranes such as this, crashed machines were rapidly removed from runways, helping the war forward to victory.

Le Tourneau's machine that " lays " houses is creating interest throughout the world. A huge mould of the required shape is filled with concrete, which, when dry, can be deposited wherever required by the special conveyor shown above, which then lifts off the mould, and the house emerges as lower picture, only needing finishing touches.

Giving a lead in aggressive Gospel witness, the Foundation has purchased and equipped a Gospel Bus, at a cost of fifteen thousand dollars. This magnificent streamliner of the road has living accommodation for four people, and is constantly engaged in going from place to place, cities, towns and villages being visited in turn. By means of its public address system the largest crowds can be reached with the human voice, and, on the other hand, through the distribution of Christian literature the way is opened up for individual dealing through which many lives are influenced for Jesus Christ.

It would be difficult to exhaust the many-sided ministries of the Foundation, operating through the Evangelistic Center. Through its funds, the services of evangelists, Gospel soloists and musicians, and other experienced workers, are made available to churches; a staff of missionaries is supported, working exclusively with children, both in city and country, and operating in schools, churches and homes; scholarships for training in Christian service are made available to worthy students; and churches, missionary societies, colleges, and other institutions, as well as independent workers, are assisted with gifts necessary for the efficient promotion of their ministries.

Needless to say, the fame of the Foundation has spread far and wide, resulting in a steady stream of letters soliciting help for this cause and for that, while many hopeful individuals present themselves personally at New York, and sometimes at Peoria, and are disappointed when they do not walk away with substantial checks in their pockets. Often they claim a direct command from the Lord to present their case before Mr. LeTourneau or his representatives, but are at a loss to explain why such heavenly revelations leave the other party uninformed. The letter files of the Foundation afford an interesting—though somewhat depressing—study in the ingenuity, cupidity, craftiness and stupidity of some people. And the carboned replies reveal how seldom these essays in optimism achieve their desired purpose. The fact is that the LeTourneau Foundation is administered under a deep sense of stewardship and with the utmost care. There are sufficient deserving causes of proven reliability to make unnecessary the risk of indiscriminate giving.

Millions for God! It is impossible to estimate the good accomplished for time and for eternity through the Foundation, established and maintained by the consecrated wealth of God's children, Bob and Evelyn LeTourneau. There is scarcely a mission-field in all five continents where some devoted worker is not grateful for assistance given through this means, or a nation under heaven in which souls have not been challenged with the Good News of God's love in Christ as a result of money or gifts in kind donated to the missionary cause. Up and down the United States the Foundation has its representatives—men and women of God—who are faithfully presenting the Gospel to young and old. How well R. G. has lived up to his resolve: "I will do my best to be God's business man"!

Chapter XIV

A CURE OF SOULS

F OR ONE brief period in his life Robert G. Le-
Tourneau was out of business. That was in the
second half of 1927. An interesting chapter in
his career had ended, leaving him free to do something
which he had for long desired, but which until then
had been impossible. He entered the Bible Institute
of Los Angeles as a student.

People today express amazement that a man with
such heavy industrial responsibilities can add to them
an almost equally heavy program of Christian activities. There is certainly a physical problem involved,
as others soon discover who attempt to keep pace with
him; but it is not a new problem. From that memorable day when he heard the call to be "God's business
man", R. G. LeTourneau has refused to allow designing
and producing earth-moving machinery to be an excuse
for abstention from personal Christian service, and
has fulfilled a dual program of astonishing proportions.

For the past ten years his schedule of week-end
engagements in all parts of the United States has made
it impossible for him to localize his service to any
particular community or place of worship. But at
Stockton, and for a while at Peoria, he and Mrs. Le-
Tourneau threw themselves with all the vigor of which
they were capable into church work, and particularly

into ministries among young people. The friends of Bethany Missionary Church, East Peoria, recall with gratitude the service rendered in the capacity of Sunday-school superintendent by Mr. LeTourneau from February, 1936, in spite of the fact that he was then carrying all the responsibilities incidental to erecting a new factory. The present church building bears testimony to this happy co-operation, being the gift of Mr. LeTourneau. That he was also its designer is self-evident, for Bethany Missionary Church is an all-welded steel structure, and for that reason, as its members believe, unique in all the world.

It was to equip himself for such service as this that R. G. entered BIOLA in 1927. There he met Marion Reynolds, a specialist in industrial evangelism, through whom he received his introduction to factory meetings. This direct Gospel approach to men, during the hours of their employment, appealed to R. G.'s practical mind, and when some years later he was engaged in constructing the highway from Boulder City to Boulder Dam, he invited Mr. Reynolds to set up an evangelistic program in his construction camp. The Boulder Dam project was memorable in more senses than one. Financially it was ruinous, but evangelistically it was a success, and the experience gained committed R. G. to maintain and extend Gospel testimony among his employees from that time forward.

As business prospered, and his staff increased, opportunities were provided for all employees to hear the Christian message under the company's auspices. At

Stockton, and later at Peoria, visiting speakers were invited at intervals, sometimes for a day's meetings, and at other times for as long as a week's campaign. There was no definite program, but these evangelistic events more or less depended upon the availability of suitable speakers. If a man with a message was in the district his services were secured, the meeting was announced throughout the plant, and invariably he had a substantial audience to address. Rarely were such meetings held without evidence of their value in lives yielded to the Lord Jesus Christ.

In the year 1941 this work of industrial evangelism was carried an important step forward by the appointment of Plant Chaplains, with responsibility for the spiritual welfare of LeTourneau employees both in the factory and out of it. Gospel meetings now passed under their direction, and became a weekly event at each of the plants, being repeated where necessary for the benefit of each shift. At Peoria, for example, four meetings are held, two for day and two for night shifts. In this way, every member of the staff has an opportunity to hear the speaker for the week.

Attendance at shop meetings, as they are usually called, is voluntary, although they are held during company time. What happens is that, on the blowing of a whistle, all work ceases, such machinery as can be stopped is switched off, and the workers make their way to the canteen, where appropriate music is already being provided. The meeting lasts for thirty minutes, and in addition to congregational singing and the address, there is usually a soloist or quartette to add interest and appeal to the occasion. All expense is borne by the company, and, it may be added, none is spared to ensure the co-operation of the best Gospel preachers, vocalists and instrumentalists. Most of the best-known figures of the American platform and pulpit have at some time or other taken part in LeTourneau shop meetings.

What of the results? Mr. LeTourneau believes that industrial evangelism brings a return in greater efficiency among the workers, an opinion which is shared by many members of his management. There is an uplift value in the thirty minutes of devotional singing and listening to which all members of the staff are invited, and in consequence nerves are steadied, anxieties soothed, problems made to appear less serious, and the logical result is a better workman. But this is only incidental to the real purpose. When asked "What is the connection between evangelism and business? Do you think it builds up the morale of your organization?" R. G. replied: "Not only the morale, but the morals also. We're trying to get men to believe in Jesus Christ, and better morale is only a by-product which is thrown in free."

"Trying to get men to believe in Jesus Christ"—that is the supreme objective of the shop meetings, and it is an objective that is being realized. Here is a man who was a top-sergeant in the U. S. Army, but who unfortunately learned other things besides soldiering, and paid the penalty by spending several months in hospital. He returned to civilian life as a machine operator in one of the LeTourneau factories, and began to attend the shop meetings, at one of which God spoke to him and he there and then raised his hand in indication of his desire to accept the Lord Jesus as Saviour. Before he returned to his machine that day he made a clean break with the past, and began to bear a clean-cut Christian testimony, which has stood the test of time. It is unlikely that this man would have entered a church to hear the Gospel; but he heard it at work, and his life is changed and enriched in consequence.

A very interesting case is that of a Jew, who had spent years lecturing on moral uplift, and who was captivated by the story of R. G.'s business partnership with God. "This man," he said, "is practicing what I am preaching," and he decided to enter the company. The shop meetings were something with which he had not reckoned, but arguing that if the man who paid his wages arranged such meetings then it was his duty to attend, he took his seat among the other employees when the whistle blew.

"That fellow is nuts, telling us that we are sinners," was his comment at the close of the meeting, at which some faithful servant of God had insisted upon man's need of salvation. To the self-sufficient Jew such a message was at once offensive and ridiculous. Nevertheless, he continued to attend the meetings from week to week, with the result that he began to realize that his program for human improvement could not be fulfilled without divine help. The handicap of sin (which at first he refused to recognize, but later came to acknowledge) prevented moral attainment, and defeated every effort at self-reformation. Throughout a year the truth of God slowly penetrated his mind, and at a meeting addressed by Phil Saint (the Gospel "lightning" artist) he publicly declared himself a Christian.

Since then he has developed his own unique method for presenting the Gospel visually. In his unconverted days he was a magician; and he is that still, with this difference that his sleight of hand is used not only to deceive the eye but to declare the Gospel also.

"Now, where did that come from?" he will ask, producing a red silk handerchief from nowhere. "Supposing we call this handerchief sin. We want to get rid of it. Very well, we will throw it away." The red handerchief is tossed into the air, but it returns to his hand a red ball. "There you are! We haven't got rid of it at all. It has come back in a different shape—which is like sin. We think we have overcome it, but it returns, perhaps in a changed shape, but it is still sin. Is there nothing we can do about it?" And this time he juggles with it, and instead of one ball there are two in his hand. "So that's what happens when we play with sin—it doubles itself, it increases!" Thus the trick proceeds, until he produces his wand, which he calls the Gospel, and one touch of the wand is enough to make the balls disappear, and to be gone for good. The application is clear!

That life, saved and serving, is a result of the shop meetings held in the LeTourneau factories. The reality of such professions is tested, of course, in contact with other employees, so that the answer to the question: "Do the converts stand?" is not a matter of hear-say or hope-so, but of knowledge. When men declare themselves Christians before their fellow workers there can be little doubt of the genuineness of their experience or of the courage of their convictions. How grand a thing it is, therefore, when—as during the writer's visit to the factory in question—fourteen men came forward at the conclusion of a meeting in response to the appeal of the visiting evangelist!

The direction of shop meetings is only part of the work of Plant Chaplains, each of whom has his own office on factory premises, where he is available at all hours of the day to members of the staff. Each man is free, of course, to develop his own methods, but in general the chaplaincy program is the same throughout the company. By visiting through the engineering shops and the offices, and by constant accessibility, the chaplain seeks to establish terms of confidence and friendship between himself and his flock. He makes it known that his counsel is available at all times, and that in emergencies he may be called upon to render all the help of which he is capable. When employees are sick he visits them; when bereaved he writes to them and where possible calls to express his own and the company's sympathy, and to commend the stricken hearts to God; when homes are blessed with the gift of children he is there to turn the parents' thoughts into words, and to praise God for His goodness and bespeak His favor; and in cases where the service of no other minister is available he is pleased to officiate in the glad as well as the sad events of life.

In times such as these when, in America as in Britain, a large percentage of the population is out of fellowship with the churches, the importance of such work cannot be exaggerated. Indeed, in both countries there is an increasing awareness of the value of industrial chaplaincies, which seem likely to be employed on a much more generous scale than hitherto. It cannot be claimed that R. G. LeTourneau was first in his field of aggressive evangelism, but surely it is true that in the degree of co-operation which exists between management and chaplains the company which bears his name is unique. It means more to the chaplains than can be put into words to know that the President of the company is one hundred per cent behind them in their endeavors to present the full Gospel and to win men to Christ.

It will be of interest to visit each of the LeTourneau factories in turn in order to mark characteristics peculiar to each as they affect the work of the chaplain's office. Beginning at Peoria, which has the largest staff and is the only plant to be situate within city limits, we learn that the chaplain began as a welder in that actual factory, but later received a call to Christian service, and after training entered upon a pastorate. The invitation to return to his former place of employment was only accepted after considerable hesitation, but what were feared as possible disadvantages have turned out to be advantages, and today this man of God declares: "I would not change jobs with any pastor."

Thursday is shop meeting day at Peoria, and, as already mentioned, because of the size of the staff, and the day and night shifts, it is necessary to hold four sessions. The chaplain has little time for other duties on Thursdays, with speakers and soloists to meet and entertain, and probably to send on their way at the close of the day. In fact, with so large a "parish" to care for, every day is heavily committed, and none is likely to pass without several visits to employees' homes and to city hospitals out of solicitude for the sick. Latterly, the chaplain has made use of the local radio station for Gospel broadcasts, and among the churches of Peoria and district he is in constant demand for both Sunday and week-night engagements. Certainly, the Peoria chaplain did not exchange a church ministry for factory evangelism in order to have an easy time!

At Toccoa there is a smaller community to care for, but since it has grown up around the plant to which it is intimately related, there is scope for considerable pastoral visitation. Most of the surrounding houses are occupied by LeTourneau employees, to whom the plant chaplain is a welcome visitor, and never more than in times of emergency. Being a man of varied gifts, he has made a unique place for himself in the esteem of the LeTourneau staff and their families. He plays baseball with the men, he teaches singing to the girls, and to all he is a messenger of Christ, fulfilling among them a ministry of encouragement, of comfort and of exhortation.

Down here in Georgia, Mr. LeTourneau has built his own radio station (WRLC), the main purpose of which is the dissemination of the Christian message, for which program the Toccoa chaplain is responsible. Each day there are three broadcasts under his direction: "The Family Altar" before breakfast, a mid-morning session of favorite hymns, and at 4 p. m. the "Old-fashioned Gospel" when the news of salvation in Christ is sent forth over a wide area. Other Christian agencies use the station during the day, and on Sundays ninety per cent of the time is occupied by local churches, including the Presbyterian Church of Toccoa, of which Dr. R. A. Forrest, of the Toccoa Falls School, is pastor.

The need for an assistant to the Toccoa chaplain will be readily appreciated, and the two men together find plenty to do to occupy their time. An interesting development of this chaplaincy, to which reference has already been made, is the inauguration of an annual Bible Conference, held in the auditorium of the Lake Louise Hotel, and offering opportunity for Christian instruction and fellowship amid the delights of mountain scenery.

Continuing our journey to Vicksburg, we find a new and distinct community gathered around the factory,

separated from Vicksburg itself by eleven miles. Here,
then, it was inevitable that the chaplain should develop his ministry along pastoral lines. At Vicksburg,
in fact, the plant canteen is in demand on Sundays for
morning Sunday School and a Gospel meeting at night,
there being no other place of worship within reasonable
distance. For both meetings, company buses are sent
out into the districts along the Mississippi River to
bring in children and adults, who otherwise would find
it difficult to attend any Christian assembly. In the
afternoons, as many as 100 to 125 boys and girls are
brought together for Bible teaching, and the evening
service is always well attended. Over $400 have been
contributed to Missions in a year from offerings received at this meeting.

If the chaplaincies at Peoria, Toccoa and Vicksburg
vary in character in response to local conditions and
needs, the Longview chaplaincy (shared by two men)
is different again, for here, in addition to the employees
of the factory, we have a student body attending the
LeTourneau Technical Institute, consisting of hundreds
of ex-servicemen. The weekly program of meetings
provides for five among the students (also attended by
students' wives and by the administrative staff of R. G.
LeTourneau, Inc.—a fine congregation rejoicing the
heart of any Gospel preacher) and two additional meetings among the factory staff. In addition, Longview
has a well-attended Bible Class on Monday evenings,
held under the auspices of the chaplains' office, but conducted by one of the Christian men in the plant.

But these meetings are only the more public part of the chaplains' duties, which, by reason of the circumstances, include more personal work than elsewhere in the organization of the company. Dormitory tours, for the purpose of contacting the single men, furnish splendid opportunities for getting to grips with ex-G.I.s on subjects of first importance; and as confidences are won these fine young fellows, who have seen war service on so many fronts, recognize the chaplains as sincere friends and reliable counsellors. In time, they make their way with their questions, their problems, their burdens to the chaplains' private offices—and there many are introduced to Him who is the Architect of true manhood.

Thus briefly we have surveyed the work of the chaplains, and yet adequately enough to demonstrate the possibilities for good, the opportunities which are presented, and the scope for initiative which is afforded. Each of the chaplains could elaborate this record with his own stories of lives transformed, of homes saved from discord and disaster, of industrial misfits who, after spiritual adjustments, became good employees, of despairing men and women finding the secret of hope, of erring youths saved from persistence in wrong-doing, and of the Gospel demonstrated afresh as "the power of God unto salvation to every one that believeth".

Chapter XV

THE CALL TO TESTIFY

O NE YEAR after he had commenced his new factory at Peoria, R. G. LeTourneau was invited to speak at a dinner of the Association of Commerce. He was not a man to seek such occasions, looking upon speech-making as something to be avoided whenever possible; but as a newcomer to the city he could do no other than respond to the courtesy of this invitation, and in this spirit he rose to take his call.

Suiting his remarks to the character of the evening, he began his speech with a review of the business conditions and prospects, proceeding to outline his own program for constructing earth-moving machinery. He told his audience why he had chosen to transfer the administrative center of his company from California to Illinois, and then added, with that natural sincerity which has endeared him to so many people: "I'm glad to be here in Peoria, too, because I find so many others in this city who love the Lord Jesus Christ."

There are some men who intrude religion into their public utterances either from a sense of duty, or to appeal to sentiment, and who do it with such clumsiness that it would almost be better not done. With R. G., however, spiritual interests are all the time predominant, with the result that his avowals of Christain discipleship bear the hall-mark of genuineness, wherever and whenever made.

At Longview, Texas, on the occasion of the official opening of the new Gregg County Airport, notables from all parts of East Texas were there, and one after another addressed the assembled crowd with words of formal appropriateness. Then the chairman called upon Robert G. LeTourneau, as a leading local industrialist and a frequent user of the airport, to speak. Advancing to the microphone, R. G. bore testimony to the Lord Jesus in the first hundred words he uttered, and he did it with such winsomeness that we all knew he spoke from his heart. Using a minimum of words he made a maximum impression.

It was just like that at the dinner in Peoria, in 1936. His expression of pleasure in finding so many Christians in the city was followed by a reminder that the founders of the United States were God-fearing men, with the added comment that if America was to continue to prosper it must serve the God of its fathers.

Next day, several local ministers telephoned him. His testimony before the Association of Commerce had made them happy. Would he be willing to come to their churches, and say the same things from their pulpits? For these things (said the ministers) needed saying, and were never more effective than when spoken by laymen.

And that was the beginning of a program of week-end engagements which has continued for ten years, and looks like going on for another ten, if the Lord grants necessary strength to His servant. As R. G.'s reputation as a speaker spread, requests for his services began to come in from far and near, and wherever he went large and oft-times overflowing congregations gathered to listen. By the summer of 1938 correspondence on the subject of meetings assumed such proportions that it became necessary to seek a suitable person to organize his engagements, which was how R. G. came to meet Dr. Harold Strathearn, who, as already mentioned, now directs this important ministry.

Perhaps a personal impression of one of these weekends would best convey their method, their opportunity, and their sometimes amazing results. Your author reached New York on a Friday afternoon, having disembarked at midday from the *Queen Elizabeth*. A telephone call to Dr. Strathearn produced the information: "We are leaving this evening for Detroit to join Mr. LeTourneau." It was, therefore, only a few hours before I was travelling westward again, this time by train, bound for the capital of the automobile empire.

We were well into Saturday before we reached our destination, having traversed a considerable stretch of Canadian territory between Buffalo and Windsor. R. G. had, of course, flown to Detroit, so we were a complete party when, at 6:30 p. m., we made our way to Immanuel Presbyterian Church, of which Dr. Albert J. Lindsey, a leading Evangelical, is pastor. There I had my first experience of an American "banquet", provided to honor the speaker of the week-end, and also to bring local Christians together in social intercourse. After years of British austerity it was almost unbelievable to see 800 people served with turkey followed by apple pie. The guest who enjoyed it most was probably the one who had come furthest!

After the meal, we proceeded to the church itself, where a considerably augmented company assembled to hear Mr. LeTourneau's testimony. Here it was explained that the organization of the week-end was in the hands of the Christian Business Men's Committee of Detroit, who had invited Mr. LeTourneau believing that his message would be an admirable preparation for a "Christ for Detroit" Campaign which they were planning at a later date. That night firstfruits were gathered, as Mr. LeTourneau's address concluded with an appeal to men and women to dedicate their lives to Jesus Christ.

It was ten o'clock before the meeting was over, and close upon midnight before some of us turned into our hotel beds. At 11 a. m. the following day—Sunday —we were on the platform of the First Church of the Nazarene, where 900 people crowded out the available accommodation in order to hear what R. G. had to say. This meeting, however, and even Saturday night's was completely eclipsed by the great gathering which assembled at 3 p. m. in the Metropolitan Methodist Church, one of the largest and most beautiful sanctuaries I saw during my stay in the States. I was told that it seated 4,000 people. That may have been an over-estimate; but certainly more than 3,000 were present to listen to a plain man's presentation of the old-fashioned Gospel.

As we left in our cars for the airport, the member of the LeTourneau party who seemed least tired was Mr. LeTourneau himself. During succeeding weeks I was to accompany this man over thousands of miles in the course of his business duties and in the discharge of his Godward stewardship, and my amazement at his tireless energy was to become an outstanding impression of that privileged association. That night we went to Texas to sleep—an air journey of 1,000 miles. And the following week-end we were repeating the program at Paris, Texas, and Hugo, Oklahoma, with visits to Lima (Ohio), Fairmont (West Virginia), Ashville (North Carolina), New Bethlehem (Pennsylvania), and a whole list of other places at seven-day intervals.

What kind of message does Mr. LeTourneau bring to these great audiences, all over the United States? Essentially a testimony to God's saving and keeping grace, and arising out of that testimony a challenge to decision for Christ and devotion to Christ. "I am not a preacher," R. G. frequently says, by which presumably he means that he makes no pretence to an expository ministry. The majority of his illustrations are drawn, not from the Scriptures, but from his own experience, or from applied mechanics, in which realm he is perfectly at home. But in that his key-thoughts are drawn from the Bible (he invariably begins with a text), and his aim is the setting forth of Christ as the all-sufficient Saviour, and his ultimate purpose the glorifying of our Lord through regenerated and consecrated lives, is he not a preacher? We may put him in the succession of Noah, who made a sermon of his ship-building, and obtained recognition as "a preacher of righteousness".

How many times he has given his personal story, "Up from Bankruptcy", he probably does not know himself. There can scarcely be a state in the Union where it has not been told. Yet thousands still flock to hear it and it is seldom given without men and women coming forward at the close to yield their lives to Jesus Christ. The theme is presented under four headings—Moral Bankruptcy, Spiritual Bankruptcy, Financial Bankruptcy and Physical Bankruptcy. Toward the close, he tells of a car crash which cost the lives of two of his companions, and left him seriously maimed on the roadside, with his wife beside him.

"One member of our party was practically unhurt. He dragged me out of the wreckage first—one foot crushed, leg broken, both hips out of joint, pelvis bone fractured, a piece of bone broken off the side of the hip socket, and chest crushed. One would not believe it possible, but I did not lose consciousness. Then he laid my wife, unconscious, on my right-hand side. She was bruised and cut from head to foot. Then he laid the other living member of our party, with broken arm and collar-bone, unconscious, on the other side.

"I looked up to heaven, and said: 'Lord, this could not have happened if you had not permitted it, because I know all things work together for good to them that love God, and, Lord, I love you'. God was so near that I wasn't anxious or worried about myself, though I did think about my children. I began to give orders to Bill to see that the six children were cared for. I wasn't thinking then of money—things like money don't matter when you're facing eternity— but I did want them to have every opportunity to live for God, if Evelyn and I went to be with Jesus. Then the thought came to me: 'Why should I complain? My Lord suffered more than this for me.' I thought of Him dying with the taunts of His enemies in His ears, adding to His physical agony. And I said: 'Thank you, Lord, for bearing all that for me.' "

There are few dry eyes as the story concludes, reaching its climax in a personal appeal to look to that crucified Saviour, who clearly means so much to the speaker. That, surely, is the secret of the platform ministry of R. G. LeTourneau—that he convinces his listeners of the reality of the experience which he describes, and presents a living Christ, whom he has proved in all the vicissitudes of an overflowing life, and with whom he enjoys daily fellowship.

The evangelistic note is rarely missing from these addresses, and there are times when the speaker rises to heights of Gospel appeal which move great audiences to demonstrative response. As he sits down, men, women, and children leave their seats and troop down the aisles to the front of the auditorium, confessing their need of Christ, and expressing their desire to receive Him as Saviour.

One of his employees, learning that R. G. was to speak in a city in the far west, told him about his son who lived there. "I didn't do much to help him to be a good man", this staff member confessed, a statement which R. G. himself could have elaborated, for he knew something of this man's wasted life before he gave his heart to the Lord. "I should be so happy if I knew he was a Christian," he declared, "and I am going to write and tell him about your meetings and pray that he may attend." That week-end, in the distant city, a young man came forward at the conclusion of one of the meetings and introduced himself as this father's son. "Are you a Christian?" R. G. asked him. He replied with a somewhat pugnacious negative. "Wouldn't you like to be a Christian?" R. G. continued, ignoring the man's tone, and telling him how many tears had been shed for him. Before R. G. went to bed that night he had heard this man acknowledge Christ as his Saviour, and he was able to take the good news home next day.

Although many conversions attend Mr. LeTourneau's spoken testimony, making none happier than himself, he is not primarily an evangelist, but he is conscious of a call to challenge Christians with their responsibilities. Many of the stories which he tells have this in view. A frequently-repeated incident concerns his early associations with Henry J. Kaiser. During the winter of 1926-27 he had worked for Kaiser, over-hauling his scrapers, and the Big Man wanted the relationship to continue on a more intimate basis. He suggested taking over the LeTourneau concern, lock, stock and barrel. R. G. accordingly made an inventory of his equipment, pricing each item on his own valuation, and submitting the list with the expectation that (1) some of the equipment would be rejected as unwanted, and (2) his prices would be pared down. To his surprise, however, the list was accepted as it stood, and the full price paid.

"I was amazed and a bit puzzled," says R. G., telling the story. "But when I thought things through I saw that this man was clever. He wasn't going to have me working for him by day, and then going home to do jobs for myself in my own workshop. He wanted all there was of me, so he bought me right out. And that's how God wants us to serve Him. The Bible says 'no man can serve two masters,' but the trouble with so many Christian people is that they are trying to do just that. And it won't work."

There are few auditoriums, however large, in which Mr. LeTourneau cannot make himself heard. He has a great voice with which he could easily be independent of the amplifying apparatus which is invariably installed in American public buildings, and he can use it to tremendous effect. But when he is really getting to grips with his audience he descends to more confidential tones, leaning across the desk in front of him, and beating a tattoo on the floor all the while with his foot. Then his voice becomes tender and wooing, and as he speaks of his Lord and Master influences are let loose which bring returns for eternity.

As a layman engaged in Big Business, Mr. LeTourneau naturally makes a strong appeal to men, and he is frequently asked to speak to exclusively male audiences, not always convened under religious auspices, but nevertheless affording opportunity for delivering a spiritual message. A typical occasion was the National Convention of the National Association of Foremen, held in Los Angeles, in the autumn of 1947. There, before a great crowd of men assembled from all parts of the United States, he was able to expound his ideas on industry with a strong admixture of scriptural truth calculated to send his listeners away with much food for thought.

For many years Mr. LeTourneau has given his generous support to organizations which exist to stimulate and promote the testimony of laymen. He was International President of the Gideons in 1940-41, and on the occasion of his induction to office he used words which express his views on the importance of a forceful lay witness. Speaking from Heb. 4:12, where the Word of God is described as "quick, and powerful, and sharper than any two-edged sword" (a text chosen because of its applicability to the principal activity of the Gideons in circulating the Scriptures), Mr. LeTourneau said:

"Just as God called men of old to do certain things, I believe He is today making that call more especially to commercial men to witness that the Gospel is still the power of God unto salvation. We commercial men have no conflict with the preachers who are preaching salvation through the blood of Christ. But when we laymen, who rub shoulders with people in the world every day, tell them that Jesus Christ is the solution to all our problems, they sit up and take notice, for they can't say of us, as they sometimes say of the preachers, 'They get paid for it!'

"When we sell machinery, we have to demonstrate to the contractors that it will do the job. So, in order to get the Gospel over to this unbelieving world, we laymen must be demonstrators, both by our lives and with our lips. It is up to us laymen to show the people of the world that the Gospel is practical. Many of us are proving daily that Christianity and business *will* mix. That God is calling more and more business men to witness to the power of the Gospel is one of the most encouraging signs of the times."

The National Laymen's Evangelistic Association is another organization to which Mr. LeTourneau has given much assistance, and his interest in the Christian Business Men's Committees has been acknowledged by his election as International President.

The CBMC, which unites men in aggressive evangelistic witness, is gaining strength throughout the United States, and reaching out to other countries where its interdenominational program is welcomed.

By filling executive offices of this sort Mr. LeTourneau promotes a cause which is very near to his heart, but his greatest contribution is unquestionably his own itinerating ministry with its constant emphasis upon the responsibility of Christian stewardship. With every artifice in his power—personal reminiscence, apt illustration and humorous anecdote—he drives home his point that "we mustn't leave all the business of the Church to the preachers. We laymen have got our part to play, and if we love the Lord we shall want to do it".

Something more must be said about his employment of humor. Mr. LeTourneau loves good stories, and is a master at passing them on. Possessing a gift for mimicry, he soon gets the response of laughter from his audience, and never more than when he assumes the Negro dialect. I have seen Negroes themselves as heartily amused over his intonations as white people, and as ready, too, to appreciate the application of his humor, for it is never pointless.

A story he tells when seeking to arouse Christians to assume their reponsibilities concerns a town boy who went to help a farmer. They set to work together sawing logs with a cross-saw. Gradually, the boy's contribution became less and less, until at last the farmer exclaimed: "Say, boy! I don't mind you *ridin'* on the saw, but don't drag your feet!" When the laughter has died down, R. G. will add: "Some of us are leaving all the work to the minister, and riding on the saw. Yes, and some of us are dragging our feet." By such painless methods great truths are often driven home.

He has a keen sense of the dramatic, and can convey his own feelings of excitement to his audience. There is an incident he relates to illustrate the importance of demonstrating a faith that works. "Do we act as though we believe God?" he will ask, and continue: "Can people who know us say: 'I believe in Christianity, because I have seen it work'? That is what God needs today. Let me tell you of what happened on one occasion in North Georgia. I was trying to convince a man of the possibilities of one of my machines, and he wasn't easy to convince. Perhaps somewhat rashly I said to the driver: 'Take her to the top of that hill.' He was a wise fellow, and took a good sweep before tackling the grade. Then up and up he went, covering the yards like nobody's business. We saw him slowing down, and knew he had changed into second gear. That carried him further, but once again he was losing speed, and had to get into bottom gear. Would he make it? He was not far from the top now, but he was so slow that he was nearly stopping. If I could have got behind him I would have *poo-oo-ooshed* him over"—and spreading himself across the platform R. G. supplies the necessary action, while his listeners hold their breath in anticipation. "A few more inches! Will he do it? I almost wish that I hadn't sent him on that fool errand. Now he's nearly there. Yes! He's going to make it! *He's done it!* He's over the top!"

Of course, he got the order on that demonstration; and in rehearsing the story he never fails to leave in his hearers' minds a sense of the necessity that men and women who profess to be Christians should convince the world of the reality of their experience by lives that are powered by the Holy Spirit.

The message which, week by week, R. G. LeTourneau takes to audiences all over the United States is also delivered to his own employees. At intervals he is scheduled as speaker for the shop meetings in his factories, and before those who know him best he bears the same testimony to Christ as Saviour, Friend and Lord. On these occasions, however, he seems to open his heart more completely, for these are people in whom he can confide, and he wants them not only as followers of his Master, but as fellow-laborers in his wider ministry, prayer-partners, who, knowing his temptations and weaknesses, will be all the more faithful in commending him to the sufficiency of God.

"I believe my Bible"—he is speaking to the Peoria staff now—"and I believe the story of creation because it is a reasonable explanation of things. Look at my big 300 horse-power *Tournapull*. Could anyone be so silly as to think that it just happened like that? Of course not. So, when we look at the world, we know that there must have been a Mind and a Maker behind it. But I believe my Bible, too, because I know the Author. My Lord made Himself of no reputation, and came down to this sin-cursed world, and took His place among men even though He was God. And He went to the cross of Calvary that He might save your soul and mine. He died to purchase our forgiveness, and as we accept that forgiveness our sins are washed away."

So, to the men and women on his pay-roll, he presents Christ. And then, lest in any wise he should be a stumbling-block, he confesses before them his shortcomings, and asks their prayers. "I believe in prayer. Maybe I don't spend as much time on my knees as some Christians, but I certainly pray plenty during the day. I have need to ask the Lord to keep me straight—yes, I may as well be honest, to keep me from 'blowing my top'. I believe prayer helps, and I want you to pray for me, that I may not fail my Lord."

There was at least one present that day who felt that R. G. never had a bigger moment.

Chapter XVI

GOING PLACES

ALTHOUGH no machine built in the LeTourneau factories has a maximum speed exceeding twenty-five miles an hour, the designer and proud parent of earth-moving juggernauts has always been a lover of speed. In those far-away irresponsible days before the motor-mechanic had turned his thoughts to more serious things, he went in for speed for speed's sake. Not even a broken neck deterred him from automobile racing; and (let it be no more than whispered!) there are times even now when he is liable to mistake a state highway for a speed track, as he puts his car through its paces.

R. G. LeTourneau would never agree with Robert Louis Stevenson that "to travel hopefully is a better thing than to arrive". With him arriving is the thing that matters—reaching his destination with as little delay as possible, and then on to the next task. This was his principle when business mainly occupied his time; and as more and more demands were made upon him for preaching the Gospel he came to set an even higher value on any conveyance which transported him from one point to another with a saving of minutes.

Until May, 1937, he used cars for his journeys. In that month, however, occurred the road accident to

190

which reference has been made in the preceding chapter. The driver of an oncoming automobile was seen to turn round to speak to a back-seat passenger, and in a split second his vehicle came careening across the road out of control. Five people were killed in the ensuing collision. Among the resolves made by R. G. during his convalescence was that in future he would go in for air transportation. It would not only be faster. It would be safer.

He purchased his first airplane, a single-engine Waco with accommodation for four, that year, and was soon wedded to the idea of flying. Not only could he travel quicker that way, or cover a proportionately longer mileage, but he also discovered that an airplane made an admirable office in the clouds, where he could work out new designs and thrash out obstinate problems without fear of interruption. Those who have flown with him know how—apart from intervals of relaxation when he is studying the comfort of the rest, or regaling them with humorous stories, or pointing out some place of interest below— he is busy with pencil and protractor. It is typical of the man that on the same sheet of paper on which he has worked out a knotty engineering point will be found an outline for his next Gospel address.

Since that first purchase he has acquired a number of 'planes, some for the use of the Company's service mechanics, and others for his own purposes. Most of his own flying has been done in two Lockheed machines—a "Lodestar" and a "Twelve"—although his latest acquisition, a Douglas A-26 military attack-bomber, quickly became his personal choice by reason of its speed. It can fly at nearly 400 miles an hour, and has a cruising speed of 300 miles an hour,—"the fastest thing," as R. G. will tell you, "short of a jet."

It was, of course, the possibility of air travel which induced him to decentralize his plants, by jumping from the Middle West to the Deep South. Apart from the airplane it would not be possible for him to carry out his amazing weekly schedule, which may easily add up to 5,000 miles, covered in the interests of business and of the Kingdom of God. Let us take as a typical week the days which followed the week-end in Detroit already described.

Leaving Detroit in the evening, we flew first to Peoria, where some of our party left the 'plane. These were Peoria employees who had been guests of Mr. and Mrs. LeTourneau for the week-end, enjoying the pleasures of the flight to and from Lake Erie, plus the spiritual advantages of the meetings. It is a practice of the LeTourneaus to take such guests with them whenever there is available accommodation in the 'plane, and this is typical of their thought for others. On such occasions, boxes of delicious candies show the thoroughness with which such plans are made.

Taking off again, the "Lodestar" continued its journey to Texas, a total distance of about 1,000 miles. It was late when we arrived, and we took to our beds without delay, knowing that we must make an early start the next day. We were up by six o'clock, and after a hurried breakfast motored out to the Longview (Gregg County) Airport where the "Lodestar" was warming up in readiness for a hop into Arkansas, to take R. G. to the Commencement Exercises of the John Brown University, at Siloam Springs, due to begin at nine.

After the function, at which Mr. LeTourneau addressed the assembled student body and the guests of the day, we remained only long enough to eat, and took to the air soon after midday, bound once more for Peoria. Here, at the largest of the plants, the President of the Company usually spends two days a week, but on this occasion we remained only twenty-four hours, and by early evening we were in the air once more, *en route* for Toccoa (600 miles).

Wednesday was spent, as usual, with R. G. in consultation with his managers, draftsmen and technical experts, and after supper we returned to the airstrip for another evening flight, this time to Vicksburg (540 miles), arriving in the dark. There, the day's program was pretty much as at Toccoa, for before nightfall we were away in the clouds with Longview, Texas, as our destination (225 miles). So we reached Thursday night, with a whole day in front of us at Longview and a second night's sleep in the same bed. But by Saturday afternoon the 'plane engines were warming up once more, for had not R. G. to be in Paris, Texas, that evening for a "banquet" and Gospel meeting, with services the following day, first in Paris and later in Hugo, Oklahoma?

That week our total air mileage was considerably over 3,000—and by R. G.'s standards it was by no means a busy week!

Mr. LeTourneau laughs when people ask him whether he is not forgetting the law of averages, according to which the more flying hours the greater the likelihood of accident. He has great confidence in his pilots, but more in his God. He believes that the Lord can and will take care of him as much in the air as upon the ground; indeed, he goes so far as to claim that the risk of accident is less in a 'plane than in an automobile. "I have been all smashed up on the road," he says, "but I have never had so much as a scratch in the air." It is a favorite point with him that the only danger period for the flier is the final stage of his journey which he covers by car from the airport!

There is only one recorded occasion when he confessed to feeling "a bit peculiar" and that was over the prospect of a crash landing. His 'plane was nearing the airport at Anderson, South Carolina, when it was discovered that the landing gear would not come into action. All efforts to move it, both electrically and manually, failed; and there was no alternative but to send a radio message to the airport authorities to prepare for a belly landing. As the 'plane continued to circle, with its reserve of fuel running low, Mr. and Mrs. LeTourneau (for they were together) could see ambulances arriving—for them! It was certainly an unpleasent moment; but the machine came down a few minutes later, and slid along the turf to a standstill without anything more serious than a few jolts for its passengers.

Flying in all weathers has made Mr. LeTourneau accustomed to occurrences which can be alarming to the tyro, as, for example, the severe poundings which a storm can administer to a 'plane. On one occasion, flying from Peoria to Longview, we encountered a sharp storm which threw the ship about like a cork in a rough sea. Finding it impossible to maintain my equilibrium in the forward position which I was occupying, I retired to the rear of the 'plane, where I expected to find R. G. He was not in his usual seat, but a moment later I saw him. He had gone as far into the tail as he could get, and had more or less securely wedged his large body in a position from which no sudden ascent or descent could dislodge him. And he was grinning broadly! I have seldom derived more comfort from a smile.

The story is told of a rough trip from Peoria to Schenectady, New York, for a week-end preaching engagement. Although the 'plane was never under any great strain, it received quite a buffeting from crosswinds, and was considerably tossed about. Upon reaching the destination, R. G. jumped out of the machine, shook the wings thoroughly, and remarked to the pilot: "Better take a look at the wing bolts. That trip was rough enough for some to have shaken loose." The pilot admitted that this was the first time his map-case had continually bounced into his face.

When there are other passengers flying with him, Mr. LeTourneau is an interesting and reliable guide. He delights in pointing out landmarks, for which he has a remarkable memory. If, while busy with paper and pencil, his help is asked to identify a certain tract of country over which the 'plane may be passing, he rarely hesitates before giving an answer—and in nine cases out of ten he is right. When America's vast distances are realized, this is a considerable achievement.

Landing grounds constitute a problem to a man whose journeys frequently take him to out-of-the-way places. The United States is sufficiently air-conscious for most towns of any size to possess airports; but these are often little more than cow pastures, of inadequate length for his more powerful machines to land. On his routine journeys he has made his own provision by creating an air-strip at Toccoa (his earth-moving equipment literally sliced off the top of a hill for the purpose). A second strip is under construction at Vicksburg, where, in the meantime, a meadow is made to serve. The first time the Douglas A-26 was brought in here there was considerable doubt whether the pilot would be able to make the landing, particularly since there had been heavy rain. He did it, however, with a hundred feet to spare, and suggested that this surplus ground should be sown with corn! Under his breath he was heard to remark that he was half-way across that field before he was sure that he would not have to take off again.

At Longview and Peoria there are good commercial airports, and at the latter Mr. LeTourneau erected a hanger costing $50,000, which he presented to the city. This airport, however, is some miles out of Peoria, and R. G. is looking forward to the time when he will be able to bring his machines down on a private air-strip adjoining his factory in all weathers, a facility now possible only in the summer.

Ever since Mr. LeTourneau took to the air himself he has been an advocate for missionary aviation, expressed in generous gifts for the purchase of 'planes for use in various mission fields. To date three airplanes have been given to the mission field through the Foundation, by means of which the Gospel has reached men and women who otherwise might not have heard.

Are airplanes the one luxury which R. G. permits himself? Not if the dictionary definition of "a thing desirable but not indispensable" is accepted. The prodigious program which he carries through would be quite impossible apart from air travel. Without his 'planes he would not be able to accept one-tenth of the calls which reach him for Gospel testimony, and many thousands of people would be denied the opportunity of hearing his challenging personal message. Mr. Le-Tourneau sees in the airplane the Lord's provision, enabling him to achieve what otherwise would be impracticable; and his unselfish use of these machines demonstrates that his sense of stewardship embraces them, as it does everything else that God has given him.

The children of LeTourneau employees would certainly be sorry if R. G. ceased to fly. Every August, the chaplains of the respective plants organize parties of boys and girls, who are flown to Mrs. LeTourneau's camp for a week of healthy outdoor activities under Christian leadership. For some of the children this may involve a round trip flight of 1,500 miles, with no charge except the ordinary camp fees. Was ever privilege more generously shared?

CHAPTER XVII

ONE MAN—AND GOD

"GOD'S children are immortal while their Father has anything for them to do on earth," wrote Thomas Fuller, three hundred years ago, thus furnishing an acceptable elaboration of that briefer and better-known axiom: "Man is immortal till his work is done." Fuller's version reminds us that it is to His children that God deputes His tasks; and that they (and none but they) have solid ground for presuming upon immunity from death until the work assigned to them has been completed. "Be of good cheer, Paul," said the Lord to His apostle, when the triumph of his enemies and the end of his ministry seemed imminent, "for as thou hast testified of Me in Jerusalem, so must thou bear witness also at Rome." The lease of his life could not run out while his Master required his services.

So many times has the life of R. G. LeTourneau been spared, and on at least two occasions from what appeared to be inescapable death, that one cannot fail to see the hand of God in it. The unfolding of our story has surely established that the Lord had—and still has—a special task for his servant, of such a character that only he could do it; and in order that the program of his life might be fulfilled he has been the subject of truly amazing deliverances. The fatal automobile ac-

cident of June, 1937, in which five persons were killed,
is something to which we need not again refer in de-
tail; but it is interesting to return to Mr. LeTourneau's
childhood, and to recall some of the alarming experiences which have befallen him, and on account of
which he today gives praise to God for His preserving
mercy.

One of his earliest misadventures occurred when
swimming in Lake Superior. With typically boyish
impetuosity, he dived in without determining the depth
of the lake, and struck his head upon a rock with such
force that he laid bare his scalp. It was a hard way
of learning the excellence of the advice: "Look before
you leap"! Physically tough even in those days, he
replaced the flesh of his broken head, and walking and
running managed to reach home—five miles away.
Covered with blood, he stumbled into the house, and
fell in a state of collapse upon a couch. The agitation
of his poor mother can be imagined; but as distance
reduced the memory of the shock of that experience
she used to laugh when she recalled that, in answer
to her anxious inquiries as to what had happened,
Robert replied: "Mother, I hate to trouble you but I
guess you'll have to get the doctor." When that good
man arrived he found it necessary to put sixteen
stitches in the boy's head.

Shortly after his conversion at the age of sixteen, he
decided to go to San Francisco in search of work. His
parents were none too pleased at the decision, but at
length consented. As R. G. himself put it: "I am sure

they would have put up a fight if I had asked them a few months before; but now I was saved they knew I had something to help me and keep me straight, so they let me go." They must have regretted parting with their son when, some time later, news came through of the great San Francisco earthquake (April 18, 1906), with its heavy toll of lives; but after hours of anxiety they at last heard of his escape, although he was in the affected area.

He was rudely awakened on that April morning by the violence of the quake, which made his bed and the rest of the furniture in his room jump around like living things. Stumbling out of bed, with a sickening sensation in his stomach, he discovered that the house had sunk into the ground, and was leaning at an angle against the house adjoining, which fortunately stood. He gathered together a few personal belongings, stuffing them into a satchel, and stepped out of his upstairs window to the ground—a feat made possible by the subsidence of the house. Then he made his way as quickly as he could, through falling debris and burning buildings, to the home of friends, six miles outside the city. Here is his own reminiscence of what followed:

"From the hills back of my friend's home we and thousands of refugees watched the city burn. For several days we got our food by standing in a bread-line and taking what they handed to us. I'll never forget that first day—things were looking pretty bad, and there were hundreds of thousands homeless. Although we had shelter, where would we get food? That afternoon, Mrs. said to Mr.——: "Charlie, don't you think we had better go and visit our friends who run the bakery?" So they both went visiting; but my hostess told me when she returned that they had a somewhat cool reception. I have no doubt that their friends sensed that they were more interested in bread than in the baker!"

This incident has been used with good effect to illustrate the truth that God wants us to love Him not for what we get but for Himself. Mr. LeTourneau has received so much from God that he realizes the danger of making more of the gift than of the Giver—of serving God for gain rather than from gratitude. It is typical of his platform ministry that he is constantly emphasizing such things, which plumb the depths of Christian motive, and bring God's people face to face with the profounder issues of the spiritual life.

While in the garage business at Stockton, R. G. did a steady business fixing "cut-outs" to customers' cars, which had the result of making the engines roar—and the louder the roar the more the customers liked it! One day, he was in the repair-pit of his garage, fixing a cut-out with his welding-torch, a somewhat dangerous operation in view of the superfluous grease and oil which lay around. Sensing danger, he called upon one of his helpers (none other, in fact, than his namesake, Robert Gilmour) to stand by with a pail of water. Sure enough, the oil ignited, and from the bottom of the pit R. G. called for assistance. Picking up a bucket, the other flung its contents over the blazing engine—but the bucket held not water but gasoline! How he got out of that pit R. G. does not know, but by the time Bob Gilmour had fetched an extinguisher from thirty feet away, he had run twice that distance and returned, and already had the flames under control. When the car owner learned of the mishap—which had done little real damage to the car—he complained that it had not been allowed to burn out, so that he might have drawn the insurance!

A slight tilt of the head, which most people will recall who have seen Mr. LeTourneau, is the legacy of another almost fatal catastrophe, in which he sustained a broken neck. This happened in the days when he went in for car racing. Exactly what happened nobody knows—but the machine suddenly left the track, charged through a fence, and treated its occupants so roughly that R. G. was unconscious for forty-eight hours, and for the next two months lay with his head limp upon his shoulder. According to all the rules he should have died; but he lived, and came out of hospital an object of amazement to all who knew him.

All of which goes to prove that this man possesses unusual physical powers. His various escapades have left their mark upon his body, but have failed to put a brake upon his energies. Taller than the average and heavier than most, he nevertheless exhausts all who match themselves against his pace of living. After a few days, nine out of ten are ready to give him best. What is the secret of this tireless vitality? Many are the suggestions offered. One of his colleagues ad-

vances the opinion that he is enabled to fulfil the demands of his exacting life because he avoids worry.
Says this friend: "R. G. crams too much into his day
to have time for worry, and when he goes to bed he's
too tired to keep awake—so he still doesn't worry!"

It is certainly noteworthy that he does not neglect
his rest. He will give himself no respite from early
morning until the evening has well advanced. But,
unless there are strong reasons to keep him from his
bed, he is there by ten o'clock and his head is no sooner
upon the pillow than he is asleep. There, unquestionably, he has a recipe for good health. It should be
unnecessary to add—though the facts are mentioned
with all the commendation they deserve—that he is
an abstainer from all intoxicants and a non-smoker.

But are any of these natural explanations adequate
to account for the superabundant energy of R. G. Le-
Tourneau, which enables him to fill every day of the
week with strenuous activity—and then to do the same
the next week, and the next? Surely one of his inti-
mates reached the heart of the matter when he said:
"It is nothing less than the grace of God that keeps
R. G. going. The Lord has a job for him to do—a
bigger job than He gives most men—and so He gives
him greater strength to do it." There is no answer so
satisfactory as that, for that is the right answer.

It is sometimes maintained that no biography should
be written of the living, partly because distance lends
perspective, and again partly because absence permits
candor. Doubtless this is, by and large, a good rule.

Yet we may recall that the fame of the resurrected Lazarus brought many to see him, and that "by reason of him, many of the Jews went away and believed on Jesus". And the glorious certainty of Easter was attested, according to the Apostle Paul, by 500 eye-witnesses, "of whom the greater part remain unto this present". It is the living, contemporary witness who is convincing.

Since God's glory, and not man's, is the object of this book, a sincere attempt has been made to present a balanced picture of our subject, not withholding appreciation where that is due, but ever bearing in mind (again to quote Paul) that "we have this treasure in earthen vessels, that the excellency of the power may be of God, and not of us". The task is made easier by R. G. LeTourneau's capacity for self-criticism and by his ready admission of imperfection.

"I don't preach perfectionism," he says, "because I know that I am not perfect—and my wife knows it, too!" He is careful not to present himself, either in experience or in practice, as an example for the fashioning of other lives. "Not I, but Christ" is the key-note of all his addresses; and in his anxiety to avoid any other impression he frequently confesses the shortcomings of his life, asking for prayer that he may not mar his testimony by unwise or unworthy behavior.

For the same reason he is at pains to give glory to God for his business successes, not glossing over his mistakes or suppressing the financial difficulties which have sometimes arisen, but unfolding the whole story in order that he may declare the faithfulness of God, who is to His people "a very present help in trouble".

Among the disappointments which have come to him must be mentioned the abortive effort to start a factory in England. Located at Stockton-on-Tees, Co. Durham, it was publicly dedicated to God by Mr. LeTourneau in October, 1946, during a memorable tour of the British Isles. Unhappily, before the plant could get into production developments in the United States made it impossible to send further financial aid, and the project had to be abandoned—not, as we hope, permanently.

"Does God still run your business?" asked a cynic one day. "Yes, as much as I let Him," was the immediate answer, revealing in its frankness. There is no pretence on the part of Mr. LeTourneau to absolute conformity to the will of God, but there is a recognition of that as the ideal for every life, and the presentation of Christ as Saviour and Sanctifier, through whom erring men and women may obtain grace to fulfil the whole council of God.

There are some successful business men who, in their zeal to testify, give the impression that the rewards of the Gospel are material and immediate. Because they have been prospered in this world's goods they would seem to suggest that faith rightly exercised is certain to bring a cash payment. In contrast to these, Mr. LeTourneau sums up the principle of the Christian life as "not using God, but letting God use us". If we seek Him merely with the hope of getting something from Him, we shall suffer disappointment; but if, because we love Him, we yield ourselves to be used by Him, then we shall experience unanticipated blessings. A song often sung by Mrs. Dorothy Strathearn at R. G.'s meetings, and probably his favorite, is Rhea Miller's "I'd rather have Jesus":

> *I'd rather have Jesus than silver or gold,*
> *I'd rather be His than have riches untold;*
> *I'd rather have Jesus than houses or lands,*
>
> *I'd rather be led by His nail-pierced hands*
> *Than to be the king of a vast domain*
> *And be held in sin's dread sway;*
> *I'd rather have Jesus than anything*
> *The world affords today.*

Wealth has certainly come to R. G. LeTourneau; but he esteems less than most people the things that wealth can bring. The luxuries of life are within his reach, but he has no use for them. A congenial task, food for the day, and a place to sleep when work is done are all he asks, and he can be satisfied with them, only desiring further that opportunity for Christian service shall be added. "Two things I like most to do," he has said. "One is to design machines, turn on the power, and see them work. The other is to help turn on the power of the Gospel, and see it work in people's lives." God permits him to do both, and he is grateful and content.

Such, then, is Robert Gilmour LeTourneau, and such the work God has enabled him to do. How far his influence may yet extend, who can tell? His visit to Britain in 1946 we have already mentioned. There he bore his testimony in many large cities before crowded audiences. He has a factory now in Australia, and it may be assumed that one day he will take that great country and its continent into his itinerary.

But I will not anticipate. I have told the story of his life. I have (within the limitations of a non-technical mind) described the mighty machines he both designs and makes. I have traced his spiritual development. I have outlined the scope of his Christian witness and the program of the Foundation which he has established. And there, at least for the time being, I must leave this my TOURNATALE.